DYNAMODB AND POSTGRESQL FOR RESTFUL API DEVELOPMENT

Exploring DynamoDB and PostgreSQL For High-Performance RESTful APIs

KRISTINE ELLIS

Chapter 1: Introduction to RESTful API Development

1.1 What is a RESTful API?

In the realm of web development, **RESTful APIs** (Representational State Transfer Application Programming Interfaces) are a cornerstone for creating scalable, reliable, and efficient web services. REST is an architectural style that leverages the principles of stateless communication, uniform interfaces, and client-server interactions. The core of RESTful APIs lies in enabling communication between a client (often a browser or mobile application) and a server through a stateless protocol, typically HTTP.

At its core, REST is designed around a few key principles:

- **Statelessness**: Each request from a client must contain all the information the server needs to understand and process it. The server does not store any session information between requests, ensuring that each request is independent.
- **Uniform Interface**: RESTful APIs promote the use of standard HTTP methods—GET, POST, PUT, DELETE, PATCH—to interact with resources. These methods follow a consistent pattern, making it easy for developers to predict how to interact with an API.
- **Resource-Based**: In REST, the focus is on resources. A resource is any piece of data or service that the API can interact with. Resources are identified by URLs (Uniform Resource Locators), and actions on them are performed using HTTP methods.
- **Representations**: The resources in REST are represented as data structures, usually in the form of JSON or XML, and are transferred between client and server. When a client requests a resource, the server returns the representation of that resource.
- **Layered System**: The architecture is designed to allow components to interact through layers. Each layer can serve different purposes, such as caching or load balancing, without the client needing to know the details of the other layers involved.

A key advantage of RESTful APIs is that they are lightweight and easy to scale, making them ideal for use in microservices architectures, mobile applications, and any system requiring distributed communication.

1

For example, when a user interacts with a mobile app that requests data from a backend server (like the weather forecast), the client sends an HTTP GET request to the server, which responds with data in a structured format (typically JSON). This simple interaction is built on the principles of REST.

RESTful APIs have become the de facto standard for modern web services, powering the infrastructure behind countless applications and platforms, including social media sites, e-commerce platforms, and cloud services. Their simplicity, scalability, and flexibility make them an ideal solution for connecting applications and systems over the internet.

1.2 The Role of Databases in API Development

In the context of API development, databases play a vital role in storing and managing the data that the API handles. Whether it's user profiles, product information, or transactional data, APIs act as the bridge between a client application and the data stored in a backend database.

Here's why databases are essential to RESTful API development:

- **Data Storage and Retrieval**: RESTful APIs rely heavily on databases to provide the persistent data that APIs expose to the client. Each HTTP request made to a RESTful API typically involves retrieving or manipulating data stored in a database. For instance, a GET request might retrieve a list of all users from a database, while a POST request might insert a new user record into the database.
- **Data Integrity and Consistency**: As the API allows multiple clients to interact with data, ensuring that data is consistent, accurate, and synchronized is essential. Databases provide mechanisms such as transactions and ACID (Atomicity, Consistency, Isolation, Durability) compliance to maintain data integrity. For instance, if multiple users are updating records at the same time, the database ensures that these updates happen in a safe and predictable manner, preventing conflicts or data corruption.
- **Data Modeling**: The design of a database schema is crucial when building an API, as it defines how data is structured, related, and accessed. In relational databases like PostgreSQL, data is organized into tables, rows, and columns. In NoSQL databases like DynamoDB, data is stored in a more flexible format, often using key-value pairs or document collections.
- **Querying and Filtering Data**: When an API client requests data, the database is responsible for querying the stored data and returning relevant results. This includes using complex filtering, sorting, and aggregation operations. A RESTful

API often provides query parameters that allow clients to specify which data they want, and the database processes those requests accordingly.

- **Performance**: A well-optimized database ensures that the API remains responsive, even when handling large amounts of data. Databases offer features like indexing, caching, and optimized query planning, which can significantly improve the performance of API calls. For high-performance applications, database optimization is crucial in preventing slow response times and ensuring scalability.

- **Security and Authorization**: Databases play an important role in securing sensitive data. For example, many APIs rely on databases to manage user authentication and authorization. By integrating secure access controls, such as role-based access control (RBAC), API developers can ensure that users only access the data they're authorized to view or modify.

Ultimately, the database and the API work together to serve as the backbone of any data-driven application. While the API provides a communication layer for clients to interact with the backend, the database ensures that the necessary data is available, consistent, and secure.

1.3 Overview of DynamoDB and PostgreSQL

When it comes to building high-performance RESTful APIs, two of the most popular database systems are **Amazon DynamoDB** and **PostgreSQL**. These two databases offer different approaches to data management, and understanding their strengths, weaknesses, and use cases will help developers choose the right tool for the job.

Amazon DynamoDB

Amazon DynamoDB is a fully managed, serverless NoSQL database service provided by AWS. DynamoDB is designed to handle large-scale, high-velocity workloads with minimal setup, management, and maintenance. It is optimized for applications that require consistent low-latency performance and can scale horizontally to handle massive amounts of data.

Key Features of DynamoDB:

- **Fully Managed**: As a fully managed service, DynamoDB abstracts away much of the operational overhead, including hardware provisioning, configuration, scaling, and patching.
- **Scalability**: DynamoDB is designed for scalability. It can automatically adjust to traffic and data size, enabling applications to grow seamlessly. It provides both on-demand and provisioned capacity modes to suit different use cases.
- **Low Latency**: DynamoDB guarantees fast, predictable performance, with single-digit millisecond latency for both reads and writes, making it ideal for applications that require real-time data access.
- **Schema-less Data Model**: DynamoDB uses a flexible key-value data model, where data is stored in tables, but each item (or record) can have different attributes. This allows for rapid changes to the data model without requiring complex migrations.
- **Global Distribution**: DynamoDB is globally distributed, meaning that data can be replicated across multiple AWS regions to improve availability and performance for worldwide applications.
- **Integration with AWS Services**: DynamoDB integrates seamlessly with other AWS services like Lambda, API Gateway, and CloudWatch, making it an ideal choice for serverless applications and microservices architectures.

Use Cases for DynamoDB:

- **Real-time applications**: Games, IoT, and social media platforms that require low-latency access to user data.
- **Scalable web applications**: E-commerce and media platforms where traffic and data grow quickly.
- **Serverless applications**: Applications built using AWS Lambda and other serverless tools benefit from DynamoDB's automatic scaling and managed environment.

PostgreSQL

PostgreSQL, on the other hand, is a powerful, open-source relational database system that is widely regarded for its stability, extensibility, and rich feature set. It is used for applications that require strong consistency, complex queries, and transactional support.

Key Features of PostgreSQL:

- **ACID Compliant**: PostgreSQL is a fully ACID-compliant relational database, meaning it guarantees the safe execution of transactions (Atomicity, Consistency, Isolation, Durability). This makes it suitable for applications that require strong data integrity.
- **SQL Support**: PostgreSQL supports SQL, the standard query language for relational databases, and offers advanced SQL features, such as joins, subqueries, and complex queries, which are essential for data-intensive applications.
- **Rich Data Types**: PostgreSQL supports a wide range of data types, including integers, floats, strings, dates, JSON, and custom types. This makes it flexible for various use cases.
- **Extensibility**: PostgreSQL allows for user-defined functions, extensions, and custom data types, enabling developers to extend its functionality as needed.
- **Strong Consistency**: PostgreSQL uses a traditional table-based schema with foreign keys, joins, and relational data models. This ensures strong consistency and is ideal for transactional applications.
- **Indexing and Optimization**: PostgreSQL offers powerful indexing and query optimization features, such as B-tree, hash, GIN, and GiST indexing, to ensure fast query performance.

Use Cases for PostgreSQL:

- **Enterprise Applications**: Financial systems, customer relationship management (CRM), and enterprise resource planning (ERP) applications that require complex queries and strong consistency.
- **Data Warehousing and Analytics**: Applications that require data aggregation, reporting, and real-time analytics benefit from PostgreSQL's advanced querying capabilities.
- **Multi-tenant Applications**: Applications that require multi-tenancy support and relational data modeling are often built on PostgreSQL.

Both DynamoDB and PostgreSQL offer significant advantages depending on the needs of the application. DynamoDB excels in scalability and low-latency access, making it ideal for modern, high-velocity applications, while PostgreSQL provides a feature-rich, relational database model that is perfect for applications requiring complex queries and strong transactional support. Understanding these databases' characteristics will help developers make informed decisions when designing RESTful APIs that need to handle large amounts of data efficiently and reliably.

5

1.4 How to Choose the Right Database for Your API

Selecting the right database for your RESTful API is one of the most critical decisions you'll make when designing an application. The database you choose will influence the performance, scalability, flexibility, and maintenance of your API. To help you make an informed decision, here are several key factors to consider when choosing between DynamoDB, PostgreSQL, or any other database solution:

1.4.1 Data Model and Structure

One of the primary factors in choosing a database is the nature of the data you'll be working with and how it will be structured.

- **Relational vs. NoSQL**: If your application requires complex relationships between entities (e.g., foreign keys, joins), **PostgreSQL** may be a better choice due to its strong relational model. Relational databases like PostgreSQL are ideal when your data fits well into a structured format and requires powerful querying capabilities.
  On the other hand, if your data is more unstructured, schema-less, or changes frequently, **DynamoDB** may be a better fit. DynamoDB's NoSQL nature allows for flexible data models, including key-value pairs and document-based structures, which is suitable for applications with rapidly evolving data models.

1.4.2 Scalability and Performance

Scalability is crucial for any modern API. As your API grows, the database must be able to scale seamlessly to handle increased traffic and data volume.

- **DynamoDB** is designed for horizontal scaling. It can automatically distribute your data across multiple servers and regions, handling traffic spikes with ease. If you expect high traffic or need to scale rapidly, DynamoDB is an excellent choice, especially for real-time applications like gaming, IoT, or social media platforms.
  PostgreSQL, being a relational database, scales vertically but can still handle significant traffic with proper optimizations. However, it requires more manual intervention to scale out across multiple servers (though features like **PostgreSQL clustering** and cloud offerings like **Amazon RDS** can help). If your application has complex transactional requirements or relies heavily on complex queries, PostgreSQL may be a better choice.

1.4.3 Transactional Integrity and ACID Compliance

For applications requiring strong transactional integrity, it's essential to choose a database that provides **ACID compliance** (Atomicity, Consistency, Isolation, Durability).

- **PostgreSQL** shines in this area. Its ACID compliance ensures that your transactions are handled safely, meaning that even in the event of a system failure, your data will remain consistent and intact. This makes PostgreSQL ideal for applications like financial systems, e-commerce, and CRM platforms where data integrity is paramount.
  DynamoDB, while reliable, is a NoSQL database designed for high throughput and scalability rather than complex transactions. Although it supports basic transactional operations (via **DynamoDB transactions**), its transactional capabilities are not as rich or flexible as PostgreSQL's.

1.4.4 Query Complexity

When choosing a database, consider the complexity of the queries your API needs to execute.

- **PostgreSQL** is ideal for applications that require complex queries with joins, aggregations, and filtering. If your API needs to perform advanced data operations, such as finding records that meet certain conditions, sorting data, or grouping data across multiple tables, PostgreSQL's powerful SQL capabilities are a natural fit.
  In contrast, **DynamoDB** is better suited for applications that need fast, simple queries based on a primary key or secondary index. While DynamoDB does support filtering and querying, it is not as flexible as PostgreSQL when dealing with more advanced query patterns or multi-table relationships.

1.4.5 Cost Considerations

The cost of operating a database can vary significantly depending on its size, traffic, and usage patterns.

- **DynamoDB** operates on a pay-per-use model, where you are charged based on read and write throughput, storage, and optional features like backups. For low-traffic applications or when data grows unpredictably, DynamoDB's pricing model can be cost-effective since it automatically scales based on usage.
  PostgreSQL, on the other hand, typically runs on a reserved instance model

(whether on-premises or through services like AWS RDS). You'll need to provision capacity ahead of time, and it might be more expensive if you're running high-volume databases without optimizations. However, if your application doesn't require massive scale, and you benefit from the relational model, PostgreSQL's pricing can be more predictable.

1.4.6 Cloud Integration and Ecosystem

- **DynamoDB** is built for seamless integration with other AWS services, making it ideal for developers already embedded within the AWS ecosystem. With native support for AWS Lambda, API Gateway, and other serverless technologies, DynamoDB fits well into serverless and microservices architectures. **PostgreSQL** also integrates with cloud services, such as **Amazon RDS** and **Google Cloud SQL**. It supports integration with various cloud-native tools and can scale well when managed properly in the cloud.

1.4.7 Use Cases

- **Choose DynamoDB** if you need a database that is highly scalable, capable of handling high throughput and low-latency requests, and has a flexible schema. It's particularly well-suited for applications like:
    - Real-time data applications (IoT, gaming, sensors)
    - Social media platforms
    - Mobile apps with fast-growing and dynamic data models
    - Serverless architectures
- **Choose PostgreSQL** if you need strong transactional support, complex queries, or structured relational data. It is an excellent choice for:
    - Financial systems
    - E-commerce platforms
    - CRM and ERP systems
    - Applications requiring complex data analysis and reporting

The decision ultimately depends on your application's data structure, scalability needs, performance requirements, and complexity of queries. If you need flexibility and speed at scale, **DynamoDB** is a great fit. However, if your API requires consistency, complex querying, and transactions, **PostgreSQL** will likely meet your needs more effectively.

1.5 Setting Up Your Development Environment

Before diving into developing your RESTful API, it's essential to set up an efficient and functional development environment. A properly configured environment allows you to write, test, and debug your API with minimal friction. Whether you're using DynamoDB, PostgreSQL, or both, the setup process involves installing necessary tools, libraries, and configurations to ensure smooth development. Here's a step-by-step guide to setting up your environment for both **DynamoDB** and **PostgreSQL**:

1.5.1 Install Required Tools and Dependencies

1. **Choose Your Development Stack**: Start by deciding on the programming language and framework for building your API. Popular choices include:
   - **Node.js** with **Express.js**
   - **Python** with **Flask** or **Django**
   - **Java** with **Spring Boot**
   - **Ruby** with **Rails**
2. **Set Up Database Clients**:

DynamoDB: Since DynamoDB is a fully managed service on AWS, you don't need to install any server locally. Instead, install the AWS SDK (e.g., **AWS SDK for JavaScript** or **Boto3 for Python**) to interact with DynamoDB from your application. Additionally, you can use **AWS CLI** to manage DynamoDB resources from your terminal.

For local development, you can also use **DynamoDB Local** (an emulator that mimics DynamoDB functionality) to simulate database operations without connecting to the AWS cloud. You can run it via Docker or install it directly.

Example setup for DynamoDB Local (via Docker):

bash

CopyEdit

```
docker run -p 8000:8000 amazon/dynamodb-local
```

- **PostgreSQL**: You'll need to install PostgreSQL either locally or via a managed service like **Amazon RDS** or **Heroku**.
  - **Local Installation**: You can download and install PostgreSQL from the official site or use a package manager like **Homebrew** (Mac) or **APT** (Ubuntu).
  - **Docker**: Alternatively, you can run PostgreSQL in a Docker container for isolated and portable environments.

9

Example setup for PostgreSQL with Docker:
bash
CopyEdit
docker run --name postgres-db -e POSTGRES_PASSWORD=mysecretpassword -d
postgres

3. **Install API Frameworks and Libraries**:
   ○ For your selected programming language, install the necessary libraries
   for interacting with the chosen database:
      - **DynamoDB** SDK or ORM libraries (e.g., **Dynamoose** for
        Node.js, **boto3** for Python)
      - **PostgreSQL** libraries (e.g., **pg** for Node.js, **psycopg2** for Python)
4. **Set Up an API Framework**: Use a framework to easily set up your RESTful
   API. For example, **Flask** for Python or **Express.js** for JavaScript. These
   frameworks provide boilerplate code to quickly start routing HTTP requests and
   connecting to your database.

1.5.2 Configure Your Development Environment

1. **Database Configuration**:
   ○ **DynamoDB**: For DynamoDB, configure your AWS credentials to
     interact with the service. This can be done via environment variables or
     using the **AWS CLI** to authenticate. For local development, ensure you
     point to your DynamoDB Local instance instead of the AWS cloud
     endpoint.
   ○ **PostgreSQL**: Create a new PostgreSQL database and user with
     appropriate privileges. Configure your application to connect to the
     database using connection strings or environment variables.
2. **Set Up Development and Test Databases**:
   ○ **DynamoDB**: Use **DynamoDB Local** for local development, or create
     separate tables in your AWS account for development and production.
     Ensure that your local development environment is isolated from
     production to avoid accidental data manipulation.
   ○ **PostgreSQL**: Set up a local database and create schemas that mirror your
     production environment. It's often helpful to use migrations (e.g.,
     Alembic for Python or **Flyway** for Java) to manage database changes
     over time.

3. **Version Control**: Use a version control system like **Git** to manage your project. It's also a good practice to use **GitHub** or **GitLab** for hosting your code and collaborating with other developers.
4. **Integrated Development Environment (IDE)**: Choose an IDE that supports both your programming language and database systems. Popular choices include **Visual Studio Code, PyCharm,** or **WebStorm**. Use extensions for database management, such as **PostgreSQL for VS Code** or **DynamoDB Explorer** for easier database management.
5. **Testing Frameworks**: Set up testing frameworks like **Jest** (for JavaScript) or **PyTest** (for Python) to write unit and integration tests for your API. Ensure you include tests for database interactions, such as verifying data insertion, retrieval, and deletion.

1.5.3 Running Your Development Environment

1. **Local Server**: Run your API locally to test endpoints. Use a tool like **Postman** or **Insomnia** to make HTTP requests and inspect responses from your API.
2. **Database Access**: Ensure your application can connect to both DynamoDB and PostgreSQL, retrieve data, and handle basic CRUD operations.
3. **Debugging and Monitoring**: Use debugging tools in your IDE to step through your code and inspect database queries. Tools like **AWS CloudWatch** for DynamoDB or **pgAdmin** for PostgreSQL can also be helpful for monitoring database activity.

By following these setup steps, you'll have a fully functional development environment for building and testing RESTful APIs with DynamoDB and PostgreSQL, ensuring a smooth development process as you move forward with building high-performance applications.

Chapter 2: DynamoDB Basics

2.1 Understanding NoSQL: What Makes DynamoDB Different

The rise of big data and distributed systems has led to the emergence of **NoSQL** (Not Only SQL) databases. NoSQL databases differ from traditional relational databases in their flexibility, scalability, and the ability to handle diverse types of data. In this section, we'll explore NoSQL databases in general and what sets **Amazon DynamoDB** apart from the rest.

What is NoSQL?

NoSQL databases are a broad category of databases that don't use the traditional table-based relational model for storing data. Instead, they use a variety of data models, including key-value stores, document databases, column-family stores, and graph databases. These databases are designed to handle large volumes of data that don't necessarily fit neatly into tables and rows. They offer more flexibility in data storage, allowing for faster read and write operations on large datasets.

While relational databases like PostgreSQL use **structured query language (SQL)** and adhere to a predefined schema, NoSQL databases like DynamoDB offer more scalability and flexibility in managing **unstructured or semi-structured** data. This makes NoSQL a good choice for applications that need to scale rapidly or handle diverse data types without a rigid schema.

Core Characteristics of NoSQL Databases

- **Schema-less Data Model**: NoSQL databases, including DynamoDB, do not require a fixed schema for the data stored within them. This allows data to be inserted without needing to define a schema beforehand, making it ideal for rapidly evolving applications where data types might change over time.
- **Scalability**: NoSQL databases are designed to scale horizontally across multiple servers, which allows them to handle massive amounts of data with ease. This makes them ideal for applications with high read/write throughput or distributed systems, as they can easily scale to accommodate growing workloads.
- **Flexibility with Data Types**: NoSQL databases support a variety of data types. For example, DynamoDB stores data in key-value pairs or documents, allowing flexibility to store semi-structured data like JSON, text, or even binary data.

- **Eventual Consistency**: Unlike relational databases that typically guarantee **strong consistency** using ACID properties (Atomicity, Consistency, Isolation, Durability), NoSQL databases often prioritize availability and partition tolerance. DynamoDB, for instance, offers an **eventual consistency** model, meaning that updates to data may take some time to propagate across the system, but it ensures that the system remains available and operational even during network partitions or server failures.

What Makes DynamoDB Different from Other NoSQL Databases?

DynamoDB is Amazon's fully managed, serverless NoSQL database that provides key advantages over other NoSQL options like MongoDB, Cassandra, or CouchDB. Here's what sets DynamoDB apart:

- **Fully Managed and Serverless**: DynamoDB is a fully managed service, meaning Amazon handles all the administrative overhead such as hardware provisioning, patching, backup, and scaling. Developers don't need to worry about infrastructure management; they can focus solely on application development.
- **Integrated with AWS Ecosystem**: DynamoDB is deeply integrated with other AWS services like **AWS Lambda, API Gateway, Amazon Redshift**, and **Amazon Elastic MapReduce (EMR)**. This makes it an ideal choice for serverless applications and microservices architectures, where services need to communicate seamlessly with each other.
- **Automatic Scaling**: One of DynamoDB's most powerful features is its ability to scale automatically. With its **on-demand** capacity mode, DynamoDB automatically adjusts to handle fluctuating workloads without manual intervention. It scales horizontally across multiple nodes without the need for developers to configure scaling rules, ensuring the system remains fast and responsive.
- **Low-Latency Performance**: DynamoDB is optimized for low-latency reads and writes, with a target response time of **single-digit milliseconds**. This makes it an excellent choice for real-time applications like mobile apps, games, and IoT devices that require quick access to data.
- **Data Model Flexibility**: DynamoDB is a **key-value store** with optional support for **document-based** data models. It allows developers to store data using a flexible schema that does not require predefined tables or complex joins, as seen in relational databases. DynamoDB tables are divided into **items**, each of which has a **primary key** and can contain any number of **attributes** (fields) of different data types.

The Evolution of DynamoDB

DynamoDB's origins lie in the research paper published by Amazon in 2007, called **Dynamo: Amazon's Highly Available Key-value Store**. The paper introduced the concept of a distributed, highly available key-value store that provided eventual consistency and horizontal scaling, which later evolved into DynamoDB.

DynamoDB's ability to handle vast amounts of data and its integration with AWS makes it the go-to NoSQL solution for cloud-based applications. While many NoSQL databases require complex configurations for scaling, DynamoDB's fully managed nature and automatic scaling capabilities make it an easy-to-use solution for developers who need performance at scale without the burden of managing infrastructure.

2.2 Key Features of DynamoDB

Amazon DynamoDB is a feature-rich, scalable NoSQL database that offers a range of tools and capabilities designed to help developers build high-performance applications quickly and efficiently. In this section, we'll explore the key features that make DynamoDB stand out as a choice for developers building modern applications.

2.2.1 Managed and Serverless Database

One of the biggest advantages of DynamoDB is that it is **fully managed**. AWS takes care of all the administrative tasks associated with database management, including:

- **Provisioning hardware**
- **Setting up partitions**
- **Scaling infrastructure**
- **Backup and recovery**
- **Patching and updates**

This makes it easy for developers to focus on building their applications without worrying about the underlying database infrastructure.

Additionally, DynamoDB is **serverless**, meaning you don't need to manage servers or worry about provisioning capacity in advance. DynamoDB offers **on-demand capacity mode**, where AWS automatically adjusts the database's capacity based on traffic patterns, ensuring that your application can handle sudden spikes in demand without any intervention.

2.2.2 Scalability and High Availability

DynamoDB is designed to scale horizontally by automatically distributing data across multiple nodes, which ensures high performance even under heavy traffic. DynamoDB supports **auto-scaling**, which automatically increases or decreases throughput capacity based on application needs, allowing you to scale seamlessly without manual intervention.

DynamoDB's architecture is built to provide high availability and fault tolerance. Data is replicated across multiple availability zones within an AWS region, meaning that even in the event of a failure in one data center, your data remains accessible from another. This level of redundancy ensures that your application remains highly available and resilient to failures.

2.2.3 Flexible Data Model

DynamoDB's flexible schema design enables you to store semi-structured and unstructured data. Data is organized into tables, but each item (or record) can have its own set of attributes (fields), which means there's no need for a predefined schema. The key elements of DynamoDB's data model include:

- **Tables**: The top-level entity in DynamoDB. A table contains multiple items.
- **Items**: Each item is a collection of attributes, identified by a primary key.
- **Attributes**: Data fields that describe an item. Attributes can have any data type, including strings, numbers, binary data, and even JSON documents.

In addition to its flexible key-value model, DynamoDB supports **secondary indexes** that enable you to query data efficiently based on attributes other than the primary key.

2.2.4 Consistent and High-Performance Reads and Writes

DynamoDB is optimized for high throughput with **single-digit millisecond latency**. Its performance is predictable even under high loads, which is crucial for applications that require fast response times. DynamoDB offers two types of consistency for reads:

- **Eventually Consistent Reads**: This is the default read consistency model. The data returned by an eventually consistent read might not reflect the most recent write, but the data will eventually become consistent across all replicas.
- **Strongly Consistent Reads**: When you need the most up-to-date data, you can use strongly consistent reads. This guarantees that the data returned is the most

recent write to the table, but it may have higher latency and cost compared to eventually consistent reads.

2.2.5 Global Tables for Cross-Region Replication

One of DynamoDB's most powerful features is **Global Tables**, which allows you to replicate your DynamoDB tables across multiple AWS regions. This feature enables low-latency access to data from anywhere in the world, making it ideal for global applications that require high availability and consistency across regions.

Global Tables provide automatic replication of changes between tables in different regions. As a result, DynamoDB ensures that your application has access to the same data, regardless of the region it's deployed in, providing seamless failover and disaster recovery.

2.2.6 Advanced Security Features

DynamoDB offers robust security features to protect sensitive data:

- **Encryption at Rest**: DynamoDB automatically encrypts your data at rest using **AWS Key Management Service (KMS)**, ensuring that your data is secure even when stored on disk.
- **Access Control**: You can control who has access to your DynamoDB tables using **AWS Identity and Access Management (IAM)**. This allows for fine-grained access control to resources at the table or item level.
- **VPC Integration**: DynamoDB can be accessed within your **Virtual Private Cloud (VPC)**, ensuring that your application and database remain isolated from the public internet.

2.2.7 Time to Live (TTL) for Data Expiration

DynamoDB provides a **Time to Live (TTL)** feature that automatically deletes items from a table after a specified period of time. This is particularly useful for managing data that is temporary or no longer needed after a certain time, such as session data or cache entries. TTL helps keep your tables free from outdated data and ensures that you're only storing relevant, up-to-date information.

Chapter 3: PostgreSQL Basics

3.1 Introduction to Relational Databases

A **relational database** is a type of database management system (DBMS) that organizes data into structured tables based on a schema, which defines the relationships between different entities. The relational model was introduced by **Edgar F. Codd** in the 1970s, revolutionizing how data was stored and queried. Since then, relational databases have become the standard for managing data in many types of applications, ranging from financial systems to customer relationship management (CRM) tools and e-commerce platforms.

Key Concepts of Relational Databases

- **Tables (Relations)**: In a relational database, data is stored in **tables**, also known as **relations**. Each table consists of rows (records) and columns (attributes). Each row represents a single entity (e.g., a customer, a product, an order), and each column represents an attribute or property of that entity (e.g., name, price, order date). For example, in a customer table, one row may represent a customer's details, and columns would store information like customer_id, first_name, last_name, email, and phone_number.
- **Primary Key**: Every table in a relational database must have a **primary key**, which is a unique identifier for each row in the table. The primary key ensures that each record can be uniquely identified, preventing duplicate records and ensuring data integrity. For example, in a table of users, the user_id column might serve as the primary key.
- **Foreign Key**: A **foreign key** is a column (or set of columns) that establishes a link between two tables. It is a reference to the primary key of another table. Foreign keys are used to establish relationships between different entities, which is the foundation of relational database design. For example, in an order table, the user_id might serve as a foreign key to the users table, linking each order to a specific customer.
- **Normalization**: In relational databases, **normalization** refers to the process of organizing data to reduce redundancy and dependency. The goal is to ensure that each piece of data is stored only once and that relationships are well-defined. Normalization typically involves breaking down large tables into smaller ones and linking them via foreign keys.
- **SQL (Structured Query Language)**: Relational databases use **SQL** to query and manipulate data. SQL is a declarative programming language that allows

users to request specific information from one or more tables. SQL includes statements for querying (SELECT), updating (UPDATE), inserting (INSERT), and deleting (DELETE) data, as well as defining and modifying the database structure (using CREATE, ALTER, DROP).

Why Relational Databases Are Popular

Relational databases remain popular due to several advantages:

- **Data Integrity**: With constraints like **primary keys** and **foreign keys**, relational databases ensure data integrity, preventing inconsistent or duplicate data entries.
- **Complex Queries**: Relational databases excel at handling complex queries, especially when combining multiple tables using SQL joins. They allow for the execution of sophisticated queries that involve filtering, sorting, grouping, and aggregating data.
- **ACID Compliance**: Relational databases generally provide **ACID** compliance (Atomicity, Consistency, Isolation, Durability), ensuring that transactions are processed reliably. This makes them ideal for applications that require strong consistency and data accuracy, such as banking systems or inventory management.
- **Structured Data**: Relational databases are particularly suited for applications with well-defined, structured data that fits neatly into tables with a fixed schema. This makes them ideal for applications like accounting software, human resources management, or customer databases.
- **Maturity and Stability**: Relational databases are well-established, with decades of use and extensive support. Many have robust community and enterprise backing, making them reliable choices for large, mission-critical applications.

While relational databases have many strengths, they are not always the best choice for every use case. For example, applications with rapidly changing or unstructured data may benefit from **NoSQL** databases like **DynamoDB**. However, relational databases like **PostgreSQL** remain a top choice for applications that require strong consistency, transactional support, and complex querying capabilities.

3.2 Key Features of PostgreSQL

PostgreSQL is an open-source, object-relational database management system (ORDBMS) that extends the capabilities of traditional relational databases by supporting advanced features such as object-oriented programming concepts, extensibility, and compatibility with both SQL and NoSQL data models. Over the years, PostgreSQL has earned a reputation as one of the most robust, scalable, and feature-rich relational databases available.

3.2.1 ACID Compliance

One of PostgreSQL's most important features is its **ACID compliance**, which ensures that all database transactions are processed reliably. ACID stands for:

- **Atomicity**: Each transaction is treated as a single unit, which either completes in its entirety or does not happen at all. If there's an error during a transaction, the database rolls back the changes, ensuring data consistency.
- **Consistency**: The database must transition from one consistent state to another, meaning that all data must adhere to the defined rules and constraints (such as primary key and foreign key constraints).
- **Isolation**: Transactions are isolated from each other, meaning the changes made by one transaction are not visible to other transactions until the transaction is committed.
- **Durability**: Once a transaction is committed, its changes are permanent, even in the event of a system failure.

PostgreSQL's full ACID compliance makes it an ideal choice for applications that require strong data consistency, such as financial systems, e-commerce platforms, and customer databases.

3.2.2 Advanced SQL Features

PostgreSQL supports a wide range of advanced SQL features that make it highly suitable for complex queries and data manipulation. These features include:

- **Joins**: PostgreSQL allows for **inner, outer, cross**, and **self** joins, enabling developers to combine data from multiple tables.
- **Subqueries**: Subqueries allow developers to write queries within queries, making it possible to perform complex data retrieval tasks in a single SQL statement.
- **Grouping and Aggregation**: PostgreSQL supports aggregate functions like COUNT, SUM, AVG, MAX, and MIN, along with GROUP BY clauses, to group data and perform calculations across groups.
- **Window Functions**: Window functions allow for the calculation of running totals, averages, and rankings over a specified window of data, making them invaluable for reporting and analytics.

19

- **Full-Text Search**: PostgreSQL offers advanced **full-text search** capabilities, allowing for the efficient indexing and querying of large volumes of text data. This is useful for applications like document management systems or search engines.

3.2.3 Extensibility

One of PostgreSQL's standout features is its extensibility. PostgreSQL allows developers to extend its functionality through:

- **User-Defined Data Types (UDTs)**: PostgreSQL supports custom data types, enabling developers to create complex data structures that go beyond the standard built-in types like integer, text, and date.
- **User-Defined Functions (UDFs)**: Developers can write their own functions to perform specific operations within SQL queries. UDFs can be written in SQL, as well as other programming languages like **PL/pgSQL**, **Python**, and **Perl**.
- **Extensions**: PostgreSQL supports the use of extensions, which are pre-packaged modules that add functionality to the database. Notable extensions include **PostGIS** for geographic data, **pg_partman** for table partitioning, and **pg_trgm** for fuzzy string matching.
- **Custom Operators**: PostgreSQL allows the creation of custom operators to perform custom calculations on data. These can be tailored to the specific needs of an application.

3.2.4 JSON and NoSQL Support

While PostgreSQL is primarily a relational database, it also supports **NoSQL-like** features, including native JSON and JSONB (binary JSON) support. This allows developers to store semi-structured data alongside structured relational data in the same database.

- **JSON**: PostgreSQL allows you to store and query JSON data using a variety of functions and operators. This is particularly useful for applications that need to work with dynamic, schema-less data.
- **JSONB**: JSONB is a binary format of JSON data that supports efficient storage and querying. It provides better performance than the regular JSON data type, particularly for large datasets.

PostgreSQL's ability to handle both relational and semi-structured data in the same database allows developers to use it for a broader range of applications, from traditional

OLTP (online transaction processing) systems to modern applications that rely on flexible, schema-less data models.

3.2.5 High Availability and Replication

PostgreSQL supports high availability and replication features to ensure that the database remains available and can handle failover scenarios:

- **Streaming Replication**: PostgreSQL supports **synchronous** and **asynchronous** streaming replication, where data from the master node is continuously replicated to one or more read-only standby nodes. This improves availability and allows for load balancing by distributing read queries across multiple replicas.
- **Hot Standby**: PostgreSQL's **hot standby** feature allows you to run read-only queries on standby replicas while the primary server is still active, ensuring minimal downtime during maintenance or failure events.
- **Point-in-Time Recovery (PITR)**: PostgreSQL enables point-in-time recovery, which allows you to restore the database to any specific point in time, making it ideal for disaster recovery scenarios.

3.2.6 Performance and Optimization

PostgreSQL is designed for high performance, with several features that help developers optimize query execution and database management:

- **Indexes**: PostgreSQL supports several types of indexes, including **B-tree**, **hash**, **GIN**, and **GiST** indexes, to improve the performance of common queries, especially those involving searching, filtering, and sorting data.
- **Query Planner and Optimizer**: PostgreSQL's query planner evaluates various execution plans and selects the most efficient one, ensuring that queries are executed with optimal performance.
- **Table Partitioning**: PostgreSQL supports table partitioning, which allows large tables to be split into smaller, more manageable pieces, improving query performance and making it easier to maintain large datasets.
- **Connection Pooling**: PostgreSQL supports connection pooling to manage the overhead of establishing new connections, which is crucial for applications with high traffic.

PostgreSQL combines the power and reliability of traditional relational databases with the flexibility and scalability needed for modern applications. Its advanced features—such as full ACID compliance, complex querying, extensibility, and NoSQL-like support—make it an excellent choice for applications of all sizes. Understanding these key features will help you leverage PostgreSQL to build robust, high-performance RESTful APIs and applications.

3.3 Data Modeling in PostgreSQL

Data modeling in PostgreSQL is a critical aspect of ensuring efficient data storage, retrieval, and maintenance. PostgreSQL follows the **relational model**, meaning that data is stored in **tables** with defined **relationships** between them. The key to effective data modeling in PostgreSQL is understanding how to structure your tables, establish relationships between them, and design queries that efficiently fetch the necessary data.

3.3.1 Core Elements of Data Modeling

Tables (Relations): Tables are the fundamental structures in a relational database. Each table stores data in rows (records) and columns (attributes). When modeling your data, it's crucial to understand the entities involved in your application and how they relate to one another. For example, in an e-commerce platform, you might have tables for Customers, Products, and Orders.

Example table:

sql

Copy

```
CREATE TABLE Customers (
    customer_id SERIAL PRIMARY KEY,
    first_name VARCHAR(100),
    last_name VARCHAR(100),
    email VARCHAR(100) UNIQUE NOT NULL,
    phone VARCHAR(15)
);
```

1. **Primary Keys**: Each table must have a **primary key**, which uniquely identifies each row in the table. The primary key ensures data integrity and prevents duplication. It is typically an auto-incrementing value, like a serial type in PostgreSQL, or a unique attribute like email.

Example:
sql
Copy
CREATE TABLE Orders (

order_id SERIAL PRIMARY KEY,
customer_id INT REFERENCES Customers(customer_id),
order_date TIMESTAMP,
total_amount DECIMAL
);

2. **Foreign Keys**: A **foreign key** is a column (or set of columns) that establishes a relationship between two tables. It is a reference to the primary key of another table. This helps enforce referential integrity, ensuring that data is consistent and valid. For example, an Orders table might have a customer_id foreign key, linking it to the Customers table.

3. Attributes (Columns): Attributes define the characteristics of each entity. Each column in a table has a **data type** (e.g., VARCHAR, INTEGER, DECIMAL, DATE). When designing your schema, consider the data types that are most appropriate for each attribute and ensure they align with the application's requirements.
Example:
sql
Copy
CREATE TABLE Products (
    product_id SERIAL PRIMARY KEY,
    name VARCHAR(255) NOT NULL,
    price DECIMAL(10, 2),
    stock_quantity INT
);

4. Indexes: **Indexes** improve query performance by allowing the database to quickly locate rows based on specific columns. While PostgreSQL automatically creates an index on primary keys, you should also create indexes on columns that are frequently queried or used in **JOIN** operations. Be mindful, however, that indexes can add overhead to write operations (INSERT, UPDATE, DELETE).

Example:
sql
Copy
CREATE INDEX idx_customer_email ON Customers(email);

3.3.2 Relationships Between Tables

In a relational database, the relationships between tables define how data from different tables can be joined together to form meaningful results. PostgreSQL supports three main types of relationships:

One-to-One (1:1): A one-to-one relationship exists when each row in one table corresponds to a single row in another table. This relationship is less common but can be useful when storing information that needs to be split across multiple tables for organizational reasons.
Example:
sql
Copy

```
CREATE TABLE EmployeeDetails (
    employee_id INT PRIMARY KEY,
    hire_date DATE,
    salary DECIMAL
);

CREATE TABLE Employees (
    employee_id INT PRIMARY KEY,
    first_name VARCHAR(100),
    last_name VARCHAR(100),
    email VARCHAR(100) UNIQUE NOT NULL,
    FOREIGN KEY (employee_id) REFERENCES EmployeeDetails(employee_id)
);
```

- **One-to-Many (1:N)**: A one-to-many relationship exists when one row in a table can be related to multiple rows in another table. This is the most common relationship in relational databases. For example, a **Customer** can have many **Orders**, but each **Order** belongs to only one **Customer**.

24

Example:
sql
Copy
CREATE TABLE Orders (

```sql
order_id SERIAL PRIMARY KEY,
customer_id INT,
order_date DATE,
total_amount DECIMAL,
FOREIGN KEY (customer_id) REFERENCES Customers(customer_id)
);
```

- **Many-to-Many (N:M)**: A many-to-many relationship exists when multiple rows in one table are related to multiple rows in another table. PostgreSQL handles many-to-many relationships using a **junction table**, which stores the associations between the two tables.
  Example:
  sql
  Copy
  CREATE TABLE ProductOrders (

```sql
product_id INT,
order_id INT,
PRIMARY KEY (product_id, order_id),
FOREIGN KEY (product_id) REFERENCES Products(product_id),
FOREIGN KEY (order_id) REFERENCES Orders(order_id)
);
```

3.3.3 Normalization and Denormalization

In relational database design, **normalization** is the process of organizing data to minimize redundancy and dependency. It involves dividing a database into smaller, more manageable tables and establishing relationships between them.

Normalization is typically done in stages, called **normal forms** (NF), with each level representing a stricter set of rules. The goal is to reduce data anomalies and ensure data consistency. However, while normalization improves data integrity, it can lead to complex queries that involve joining multiple tables. Therefore, some databases may choose to **denormalize** data for performance reasons, especially in read-heavy applications.

3.3.4 Entity-Relationship Diagrams (ERD)

An **Entity-Relationship Diagram (ERD)** is a visual tool used to model the relationships between entities in a database. ERDs are useful for planning the structure of your database and ensuring that your tables and relationships are designed efficiently.

3.4 Setting Up PostgreSQL Locally and in the Cloud

Setting up PostgreSQL for local and cloud use involves several steps to ensure that you can access the database securely and perform operations like creating tables, managing data, and configuring backups. This section will guide you through setting up PostgreSQL both locally (on your machine) and in the cloud (using a service like Amazon RDS).

3.4.1 Setting Up PostgreSQL Locally

1. **Install PostgreSQL**: First, you need to install PostgreSQL on your local machine. The installation process varies depending on your operating system:
   - **Windows**: Download the installer from the official PostgreSQL website and follow the installation wizard.
   - **MacOS**: Use a package manager like Homebrew (brew install postgresql), or download the installer from the official site.
   - **Linux**: Use the package manager for your distribution (e.g., sudo apt install postgresql for Ubuntu).
2. **Start PostgreSQL**: After installation, you can start PostgreSQL using the following commands:
   - **Linux/MacOS**: Run sudo service postgresql start or pg_ctl start depending on your setup.
   - **Windows**: PostgreSQL should automatically start as a service, but you can also start it manually through the PostgreSQL Service in the Windows Services Manager.

3. **Access the PostgreSQL Command Line**: Use the psql command-line utility to interact with the PostgreSQL database.
bash
Copy
```
psql -U postgres
```

26

This will connect you to the default PostgreSQL instance as the postgres user.

4. Create a New Database: Once connected to the psql terminal, create a new database using the following SQL command:
sql
Copy
```
CREATE DATABASE mydatabase;
```

5. Create Tables and Define Relationships: You can now start defining tables, relationships, and data types in your new database using SQL.

3.4.2 Setting Up PostgreSQL in the Cloud

Cloud platforms such as Amazon Web Services (AWS), Google Cloud, and Heroku offer managed PostgreSQL databases that make it easy to deploy and scale PostgreSQL without managing infrastructure. Below, we will focus on setting up PostgreSQL in **AWS RDS** and **Heroku**.

AWS RDS PostgreSQL Setup

1. **Create an AWS Account**: If you don't already have an AWS account, sign up at aws.amazon.com.
2. **Launch an RDS Instance**:
   - Navigate to **RDS** in the AWS Management Console.
   - Click on **Create database**, then choose **PostgreSQL** as the engine.
   - Select the **DB instance size**, storage type, and other configurations.
   - Set a username and password for the database, and configure VPC settings to define the networking rules.
3. **Connect to PostgreSQL**:
   - After the database instance is created, use the **endpoint** and port (usually 5432) to connect to the instance via a PostgreSQL client, such as psql or **pgAdmin**.

Example connection:
bash
Copy
```
psql -h <endpoint> -U <username> -d <dbname> -p 5432
```

Heroku PostgreSQL Setup

1. **Create a Heroku Account**: Sign up at heroku.com and install the Heroku CLI.

2. **Create an App and Add PostgreSQL**:
bash
Copy
heroku create myapp
heroku addons:create heroku-postgresql:hobby-dev

3. **Access PostgreSQL**:
   o Use the following command to connect to the Heroku PostgreSQL instance:

bash
Copy
heroku pg:psql

4. Create Tables and Manage Data: Once connected, you can run SQL commands to create tables, insert data, and query your PostgreSQL instance.

3.5 Database Normalization and Schemas

Normalization refers to the process of organizing data in a database to reduce redundancy and dependency. The goal is to ensure that the database structure is efficient, flexible, and free of anomalies. PostgreSQL follows the principles of **First Normal Form (1NF)** through **Fifth Normal Form (5NF)**.

3.5.1 The Normal Forms

1. **First Normal Form (1NF)**: Each table must have atomic columns (each column contains only a single value), and each row must be unique.
2. **Second Normal Form (2NF)**: Achieved by ensuring that all non-key attributes are fully dependent on the primary key. This eliminates partial dependency.
3. **Third Normal Form (3NF)**: In this form, there are no transitive dependencies—i.e., no non-key attributes depend on other non-key attributes.
4. **Boyce-Codd Normal Form (BCNF)**: This is a stricter version of 3NF, where every determinant is a candidate key.

28

5. **Fourth and Fifth Normal Forms (4NF & 5NF)**: These deal with multi-valued dependencies and join dependencies, respectively, aiming for a database structure that is free from all types of redundancy.

3.5.2 Schema Design

The **schema** of a PostgreSQL database defines the structure of tables, relationships, data types, and constraints. When designing your schema, it's important to consider:

- **Data Integrity**: Define appropriate constraints (e.g., **NOT NULL, UNIQUE, CHECK**) to ensure that only valid data is inserted.
- **Indexes**: Define indexes on frequently queried columns to improve performance.
- **Foreign Keys**: Use foreign keys to enforce referential integrity between tables and maintain relationships.
- **Normalization**: Normalize your database to eliminate redundancy and ensure data consistency, but also consider the performance implications of normalization.

Chapter 4: Building a CRUD API with DynamoDB

4.1 Setting Up Your AWS SDK

Before you can start building a CRUD API with **DynamoDB**, you first need to set up the **AWS SDK** for the programming language you plan to use. The **AWS SDK** provides libraries that allow you to interact with AWS services like DynamoDB directly from your application. In this section, we'll walk through the steps to set up the AWS SDK and configure your environment to connect to DynamoDB.

4.1.1 Install the AWS SDK

To interact with DynamoDB, you'll need to install the AWS SDK for your programming language. The AWS SDK is available for multiple languages, including JavaScript, Python, Java, and others. Below are installation instructions for two popular languages: **Node.js** and **Python**.

Node.js (JavaScript)

Install Node.js: If you don't have Node.js installed, download and install it from nodejs.org.

Install the AWS SDK: Open your terminal and navigate to your project directory. Run the following command to install the AWS SDK for JavaScript:
bash
Copy

```
npm install aws-sdk
```

Set Up Your Credentials: The AWS SDK needs credentials to authenticate your requests to DynamoDB. You can set up credentials in several ways:
- o **AWS CLI**: If you've already configured the AWS CLI with your credentials, the AWS SDK will automatically use them.
- o **AWS IAM Roles**: If you're working on an EC2 instance or Lambda function, assign appropriate IAM roles for access to DynamoDB.
- o **Access Keys**: Alternatively, you can configure your credentials manually in your code or environment variables.

Test the Installation: Once you've installed the SDK, create a simple script to verify that the SDK is correctly set up. For example:

javascript

Copy

```
const AWS = require('aws-sdk');
const dynamodb = new AWS.DynamoDB();

dynamodb.listTables({}, function(err, data) {
  if (err) {
    console.error("Unable to list tables:", err);
  } else {
    console.log("Tables:", data.TableNames);
  }
});
```

Python (Boto3)

Install Python: Make sure you have Python installed. If not, download it from python.org.

Install Boto3: Boto3 is the AWS SDK for Python. Install it using pip:

bash

Copy

```
pip install boto3
```

Set Up Your Credentials: Like in Node.js, you need to configure your AWS credentials. You can use the AWS CLI, IAM roles, or access keys.

Test the Installation: Create a Python script to verify that your installation is working:

python

Copy

```
import boto3

dynamodb = boto3.client('dynamodb')
response = dynamodb.list_tables()

print(response['TableNames'])
```

31

4.1.2 Configuring AWS Region and DynamoDB Endpoint

When setting up the SDK, you also need to configure the **AWS region** where your DynamoDB instance is hosted. The region is specified either in your AWS credentials or programmatically in your SDK code.

Here's how you can configure the region in your SDK setup:

Node.js Example:
```javascript
Copy
AWS.config.update({
    region: 'us-east-1'  // Specify the region your DynamoDB is located in
});
```

Python Example:
```python
Copy
import boto3

dynamodb = boto3.client('dynamodb', region_name='us-east-1')
```

The **DynamoDB endpoint** is another configuration you may need, especially if you're using DynamoDB Local for development or connecting to a custom DynamoDB instance.

For local development, you can specify the endpoint URL like so:

Node.js:
```javascript
Copy
const dynamodb = new AWS.DynamoDB({
    endpoint: new AWS.Endpoint('http://localhost:8000')
});
```

Python:

python
Copy
```
dynamodb = boto3.client('dynamodb', endpoint_url="http://localhost:8000",
region_name="us-west-2")
```

4.1.3 Verifying DynamoDB Connection

Once the SDK is installed and configured, test the connection to DynamoDB by performing a simple operation, like listing the tables in your DynamoDB instance. If the connection is successful, you should see a list of DynamoDB tables in your account.

4.2 Creating the API Endpoints (Create, Read, Update, Delete)

With the AWS SDK set up, you can now start building the **CRUD (Create, Read, Update, Delete)** API for DynamoDB. We'll use the **Express.js** framework for Node.js as an example, but similar steps can be followed for other programming languages.

4.2.1 Set Up Express Application

Start by setting up a basic **Express.js** application to handle HTTP requests.

Install Express:
bash
Copy
```
npm install express
```

Create a Basic Server: Create a new file, server.js, and set up the basic Express server:
javascript
Copy
```
const express = require('express');
const AWS = require('aws-sdk');
const app = express();

// Body parser middleware
app.use(express.json());

const dynamodb = new AWS.DynamoDB.DocumentClient();
```

33

```javascript
app.listen(3000, () => {
  console.log('Server running on http://localhost:3000');
});
```

4.2.2 Create Operation (POST)

The **Create** operation allows clients to add new records to DynamoDB. We'll create an endpoint that accepts a POST request to add a new user to a Users table.

Assuming the Users table has the following schema:

- **Primary Key**: userID (partition key)
- **Attributes**: firstName, lastName, email

Here's how you can implement the Create endpoint:

javascript
Copy
```javascript
app.post('/users', (req, res) => {
  const { userID, firstName, lastName, email } = req.body;

  const params = {
    TableName: 'Users',
    Item: {
      userID,
      firstName,
      lastName,
      email
    }
  };

  dynamodb.put(params, (err, data) => {
    if (err) {
      res.status(500).json({ message: "Failed to create user", error: err });
    } else {
      res.status(201).json({ message: "User created successfully", data });
    }
  });
```

34

```
});
```

This POST /users endpoint adds a new user to the DynamoDB table. The request body should contain userID, firstName, lastName, and email data.

4.2.3 Read Operation (GET)

The **Read** operation allows clients to retrieve records from DynamoDB. Here, we'll create a GET endpoint to retrieve a user by their userID.

javascript
Copy
```javascript
app.get('/users/:userID', (req, res) => {
  const { userID } = req.params;

  const params = {
    TableName: 'Users',
    Key: {
      userID
    }
  };

  dynamodb.get(params, (err, data) => {
    if (err) {
      res.status(500).json({ message: "Failed to retrieve user", error: err });
    } else if (!data.Item) {
      res.status(404).json({ message: "User not found" });
    } else {
      res.status(200).json(data.Item);
    }
  });
});
```

This GET /users/:userID endpoint retrieves a user by their userID. The userID is passed as a path parameter.

4.2.4 Update Operation (PUT)

The **Update** operation allows clients to modify existing records in DynamoDB. We'll create a PUT endpoint to update a user's information.

javascript
Copy
```javascript
app.put('/users/:userID', (req, res) => {
    const { userID } = req.params;
    const { firstName, lastName, email } = req.body;

    const params = {
        TableName: 'Users',
        Key: { userID },
        UpdateExpression: 'set firstName = :firstName, lastName = :lastName, email =
:email',
        ExpressionAttributeValues: {
            ':firstName': firstName,
            ':lastName': lastName,
            ':email': email
        },
        ReturnValues: 'ALL_NEW'
    };

    dynamodb.update(params, (err, data) => {
        if (err) {
            res.status(500).json({ message: "Failed to update user", error: err });
        } else {
            res.status(200).json({ message: "User updated successfully", data:
data.Attributes });
        }
    });
});
```

The PUT /users/:userID endpoint updates the user's firstName, lastName, and email. The updated user data is returned in the response.

4.2.5 Delete Operation (DELETE)

The **Delete** operation removes records from DynamoDB. We'll create a DELETE endpoint to delete a user by userID.

javascript
Copy

```javascript
app.delete('/users/:userID', (req, res) => {
  const { userID } = req.params;

  const params = {
    TableName: 'Users',
    Key: {
      userID
    }
  };

  dynamodb.delete(params, (err, data) => {
    if (err) {
      res.status(500).json({ message: "Failed to delete user", error: err });
    } else {
      res.status(200).json({ message: "User deleted successfully" });
    }
  });
});
```

The DELETE /users/:userID endpoint deletes the user record with the specified userID from the DynamoDB table.

4.3 Handling Data in DynamoDB

When building a CRUD API with DynamoDB, handling data efficiently is key to ensuring high performance and maintaining data integrity. Data handling in DynamoDB involves operations like **inserting, retrieving, updating,** and **deleting** items in a table. Additionally, ensuring that you structure and query your data efficiently is essential for optimizing performance, especially when working with large datasets.

37

4.3.1 Inserting Data into DynamoDB

The most basic data handling operation is inserting data into DynamoDB. This is done using the **put** operation, which is used to add an item or replace an existing item in a table.

Here's an example of how you would insert a new user into a **Users** table with userID, firstName, lastName, and email as attributes:

javascript

Copy

```javascript
const AWS = require('aws-sdk');

const dynamodb = new AWS.DynamoDB.DocumentClient();


const addUser = async (userData) => {

  const params = {

    TableName: 'Users',

    Item: {

      userID: userData.userID,

      firstName: userData.firstName,

      lastName: userData.lastName,

      email: userData.email

    }

  };


  try {

    await dynamodb.put(params).promise();
```

```
        console.log('User added successfully');

    } catch (err) {

        console.error('Error adding user:', err);

    }

};



addUser({ userID: 'user123', firstName: 'John', lastName: 'Doe', email:
'john.doe@example.com' });
```

This code creates a new user entry in the **Users** table. If the table already contains an item with the same primary key, the existing item is replaced.

4.3.2 Retrieving Data from DynamoDB

To retrieve data, the **get** operation is used. You specify the primary key of the item you want to retrieve. Here's how you would retrieve a user by their userID:

javascript

Copy

```
const getUser = async (userID) => {

    const params = {

        TableName: 'Users',

        Key: {

            userID: userID

        }

    };
```

```javascript
try {

  const data = await dynamodb.get(params).promise();

  if (data.Item) {

    console.log('User found:', data.Item);

  } else {

    console.log('User not found');

  }

} catch (err) {

  console.error('Error retrieving user:', err);

}

};


getUser('user123');
```

This example fetches a user's details based on their userID. If the item exists, the data is returned; otherwise, a message indicates the user was not found.

4.3.3 Updating Data in DynamoDB

The **update** operation is used when you need to modify an existing item's attributes. DynamoDB supports updating individual attributes without modifying the entire item, which can be more efficient than replacing the whole item.

Here's an example that updates the email of a user:

javascript

Copy

```javascript
const updateUserEmail = async (userID, newEmail) => {
```

```javascript
  const params = {

    TableName: 'Users',

    Key: {

      userID: userID

    },

    UpdateExpression: 'set email = :email',

    ExpressionAttributeValues: {

      ':email': newEmail

    },

    ReturnValues: 'ALL_NEW'

  };


  try {

    const result = await dynamodb.update(params).promise();

    console.log('User updated:', result.Attributes);

  } catch (err) {

    console.error('Error updating user:', err);

  }

};


updateUserEmail('user123', 'newemail@example.com');
```

The UpdateExpression allows for flexible updates to the item. Here, only the email field is updated, while the other fields remain unchanged. The ReturnValues option specifies that the updated item should be returned.

4.3.4 Deleting Data from DynamoDB

To delete data from DynamoDB, you use the **delete** operation, which removes an item based on its primary key.

Here's how you would delete a user:

javascript

Copy

```javascript
const deleteUser = async (userID) => {

  const params = {

    TableName: 'Users',

    Key: {

      userID: userID

    }

  };


  try {

    await dynamodb.delete(params).promise();

    console.log('User deleted successfully');

  } catch (err) {

    console.error('Error deleting user:', err);

  }

};
```

```
deleteUser('user123');
```

This will delete the item with the specified userID from the **Users** table.

4.3.5 Querying and Scanning Data

In DynamoDB, you can also query and scan for items. **Querying** is more efficient than scanning, as it allows you to retrieve data based on the partition key and optional sort key, while scanning reads every item in the table.

javascript

Copy

```javascript
const queryUsersByLastName = async (lastName) => {

  const params = {

    TableName: 'Users',

    IndexName: 'lastName-index',  // Example of using a GSI to query by lastName

    KeyConditionExpression: 'lastName = :lastName',

    ExpressionAttributeValues: {

      ':lastName': lastName

    }

  };


  try {

    const result = await dynamodb.query(params).promise();

    console.log('Users with last name', lastName, ':', result.Items);

  } catch (err) {
```

```
    console.error('Error querying users:', err);

  }

};


queryUsersByLastName('Doe');
```

In this example, the query uses a **Global Secondary Index (GSI)** called lastName-index to find users with a specific last name

4.4 Implementing Data Validation

Data validation ensures that the data entering your system is in the expected format, minimizing the chances of errors and inconsistencies. For a CRUD API built on DynamoDB, you must validate both the incoming data (from API requests) and the data going into DynamoDB.

4.4.1 Validation Techniques

Here are some common techniques for validating data in a DynamoDB-based CRUD API:

1. Input Validation (at the API Level)

Before inserting data into DynamoDB, validate the input to ensure it meets the required format. This can be done using a validation library like **Joi** (for Node.js) or manually checking the data.

Example using Joi in Node.js:

javascript

Copy

```
const Joi = require('joi');
```

```javascript
// Define schema
const userSchema = Joi.object({
    userID: Joi.string().alphanum().min(3).max(30).required(),
    firstName: Joi.string().min(1).max(100).required(),
    lastName: Joi.string().min(1).max(100).required(),
    email: Joi.string().email().required()
});

// Validate data
const validateUser = (userData) => {
    const { error } = userSchema.validate(userData);
    if (error) {
        throw new Error('Invalid data: ' + error.details[0].message);
    }
};

// Example usage
try {
    const userData = {
        userID: 'user123',
        firstName: 'John',
        lastName: 'Doe',
```

```
    email: 'john.doe@example.com'

  };

  validateUser(userData);  // Validates user data

  console.log('Data is valid');

} catch (err) {

  console.error(err.message);

}
```

Here, the Joi schema ensures that the userID, firstName, lastName, and email are correctly formatted before proceeding with DynamoDB operations.

2. Data Validation with DynamoDB

You can also perform **data validation** using DynamoDB's built-in **conditional expressions**. These expressions allow you to define conditions that must be met before DynamoDB performs a write operation, such as ensuring that an item with the same primary key does not already exist.

Example using ConditionExpression **in a** put **operation**:

javascript

Copy

```
const addUserIfNotExists = async (userData) => {

  const params = {

    TableName: 'Users',

    Item: userData,

    ConditionExpression: 'attribute_not_exists(userID)'  // Ensures userID doesn't already exist
```

```
  };

  try {

    await dynamodb.put(params).promise();

    console.log('User added successfully');

  } catch (err) {

    console.error('Error adding user:', err);

  }

};
```

In this example, the ConditionExpression ensures that the item will only be inserted if the userID does not already exist in the table.

4.4.2 Validating on the Client Side

While server-side validation ensures that the data entering DynamoDB is correct, it's also a good practice to validate data on the client side (i.e., in the frontend or client application) before making the API request. This can reduce unnecessary API calls and provide immediate feedback to the user.

For instance, use JavaScript or frontend libraries like **React Hook Form** or **Formik** to validate forms and ensure that all fields conform to the expected format before sending them to your API.

4.5 Error Handling and Logging in DynamoDB APIs

Error handling and logging are essential for maintaining the health and reliability of your DynamoDB-based API. By handling errors properly, you can ensure that your API responds gracefully under failure conditions, and with logging, you can track down issues when things go wrong.

4.5.1 Common DynamoDB Errors

When interacting with DynamoDB, there are several types of errors that can occur. The AWS SDK provides detailed error messages, which you can handle to provide meaningful responses to the client.

- **ProvisionedThroughputExceededException**: This occurs when your requests exceed the provisioned read or write capacity. This can be mitigated by increasing capacity or switching to **on-demand mode** for automatic scaling.
- **ConditionalCheckFailedException**: This happens when the condition you specify for a write operation (like checking if an item exists) is not met.
- **ResourceNotFoundException**: This occurs when the requested resource (e.g., a table) is not found.

4.5.2 Handling Errors in DynamoDB API Operations

When an error occurs during a DynamoDB operation, you should handle it appropriately by sending a clear error message to the client. Here's an example of error handling in an Express.js API endpoint:

javascript

Copy

```javascript
app.post('/users', async (req, res) => {
  const { userID, firstName, lastName, email } = req.body;


  const params = {
    TableName: 'Users',
    Item: { userID, firstName, lastName, email }
  };


  try {
    await dynamodb.put(params).promise();
```

48

```
    res.status(201).json({ message: 'User created successfully' });
  } catch (err) {
    console.error('Error:', err);
    if (err.code === 'ProvisionedThroughputExceededException') {
      res.status(503).json({ message: 'Too many requests, please try again later' });
    } else {
      res.status(500).json({ message: 'Internal server error', error: err.message });
    }
  }
});
```

In this example, we handle different error scenarios and send appropriate responses back to the client. For a provisioned throughput error, we suggest retrying later, while for other types of errors, we return a generic internal server error message.

4.5.3 Logging with CloudWatch

For better monitoring and troubleshooting, use **AWS CloudWatch Logs** to capture logs of your API's interactions with DynamoDB. CloudWatch Logs can help you track DynamoDB operation results, monitor performance, and debug issues.

In your Node.js application, you can send logs to CloudWatch using the **AWS SDK**:

javascript

Copy

```
const cloudwatchlogs = new AWS.CloudWatchLogs();


const logToCloudWatch = async (message) => {
```

```
const params = {

    logGroupName: 'DynamoDB-API-Logs',

    logStreamName: 'API-Requests',

    logEvents: [

        {

            message: message,

            timestamp: Date.now()

        }

    ]

};


try {

    await cloudwatchlogs.putLogEvents(params).promise();

    console.log('Log sent to CloudWatch');

} catch (err) {

    console.error('Error sending log to CloudWatch:', err);

}

};
```

This function sends logs to CloudWatch, where you can monitor API interactions in real time.

Chapter 5: Building a CRUD API with PostgreSQL

5.1 Setting Up PostgreSQL with Flask/Django

When building a CRUD API using PostgreSQL, the first step is to set up the database and integrate it with a Python web framework such as **Flask** or **Django**. Both frameworks are popular for web development and provide excellent tools for working with PostgreSQL. This section will guide you through setting up PostgreSQL with both Flask and Django.

5.1.1 Setting Up PostgreSQL with Flask

Flask is a lightweight and flexible web framework that provides developers with the ability to build applications quickly. To integrate Flask with PostgreSQL, we will use the **SQLAlchemy** ORM (Object-Relational Mapping) for database interactions and **psycopg2** as the PostgreSQL adapter for Python.

Step-by-Step Setup for Flask with PostgreSQL
Install Required Libraries: First, you need to install Flask, SQLAlchemy, and psycopg2.
bash
Copy
```
pip install flask
pip install flask_sqlalchemy
pip install psycopg2
```

Set Up PostgreSQL: Before connecting Flask to PostgreSQL, ensure that you have a PostgreSQL instance running. You can either set up PostgreSQL locally or use a cloud-based PostgreSQL service like **Heroku** or **Amazon RDS**.
Create a new database in PostgreSQL. For example:
sql
Copy
```
CREATE DATABASE flask_crud;
```

Create Flask Application: In your Flask project, you will need to create a simple application that connects to PostgreSQL. Below is the basic structure of the application.
python
Copy

```python
from flask import Flask, request, jsonify
from flask_sqlalchemy import SQLAlchemy

app = Flask(__name__)

# Database URI to connect Flask to PostgreSQL
app.config['SQLALCHEMY_DATABASE_URI'] =
'postgresql://username:password@localhost/flask_crud'
app.config['SQLALCHEMY_TRACK_MODIFICATIONS'] = False

db = SQLAlchemy(app)

class User(db.Model):
    __tablename__ = 'users'
    id = db.Column(db.Integer, primary_key=True)
    first_name = db.Column(db.String(100), nullable=False)
    last_name = db.Column(db.String(100), nullable=False)
    email = db.Column(db.String(100), unique=True, nullable=False)

    def __repr__(self):
        return f'<User {self.first_name} {self.last_name}>'

@app.route('/users', methods=['POST'])
def create_user():
    data = request.get_json()
    new_user = User(first_name=data['first_name'], last_name=data['last_name'],
email=data['email'])
    db.session.add(new_user)
    db.session.commit()
    return jsonify({'message': 'User created successfully'}), 201

@app.route('/users', methods=['GET'])
def get_users():
    users = User.query.all()
```

```
    return jsonify([{'id': user.id, 'first_name': user.first_name, 'last_name': user.last_name,
'email': user.email} for user in users])

@app.route('/users/<int:id>', methods=['GET'])
def get_user(id):
    user = User.query.get_or_404(id)
    return jsonify({'id': user.id, 'first_name': user.first_name, 'last_name': user.last_name,
'email': user.email})

@app.route('/users/<int:id>', methods=['PUT'])
def update_user(id):
    data = request.get_json()
    user = User.query.get_or_404(id)
    user.first_name = data['first_name']
    user.last_name = data['last_name']
    user.email = data['email']
    db.session.commit()
    return jsonify({'message': 'User updated successfully'})

@app.route('/users/<int:id>', methods=['DELETE'])
def delete_user(id):
    user = User.query.get_or_404(id)
    db.session.delete(user)
    db.session.commit()
    return jsonify({'message': 'User deleted successfully'})

if __name__ == '__main__':
    db.create_all()  # Creates the database tables if they don't exist
    app.run(debug=True)
```

In this setup:

- We configure Flask to connect to the PostgreSQL database using **SQLAlchemy**.
- We define a User model that maps to a users table in the PostgreSQL database.
- We create four RESTful endpoints for **Create, Read, Update,** and **Delete** operations on the User resource.

Run the Flask Application: Run your Flask application using the following command:
bash
Copy
python app.py

Now, you have a CRUD API running on **localhost:5000**, which allows you to interact with the PostgreSQL database for user management.

5.1.2 Setting Up PostgreSQL with Django

Django is a more opinionated web framework that comes with built-in tools for working with databases, including PostgreSQL. It uses **Django ORM**, a powerful object-relational mapping library that abstracts away SQL queries.

Step-by-Step Setup for Django with PostgreSQL
Install Required Libraries: First, install Django and psycopg2 for PostgreSQL support.
bash
Copy
pip install django
pip install psycopg2

Set Up PostgreSQL: As with Flask, ensure that you have a running PostgreSQL instance and create a database for your Django application:
sql
Copy
CREATE DATABASE django_crud;

Create a Django Project: Use the Django CLI to create a new project.
bash
Copy
django-admin startproject myproject
cd myproject

Configure PostgreSQL in Django: Open the settings.py file in your Django project and configure the DATABASES setting to use PostgreSQL:

python
Copy

```
DATABASES = {
    'default': {
        'ENGINE': 'django.db.backends.postgresql',
        'NAME': 'django_crud',
        'USER': 'your_username',
        'PASSWORD': 'your_password',
        'HOST': 'localhost',
        'PORT': '5432',
    }
}
```

Create a Django App: Create a Django app to handle user-related functionality:

bash
Copy

```
python manage.py startapp users
```

Define Models: In users/models.py, define the User model that corresponds to the PostgreSQL table structure:

python
Copy

```
from django.db import models

class User(models.Model):
    first_name = models.CharField(max_length=100)
    last_name = models.CharField(max_length=100)
    email = models.EmailField(unique=True)

    def __str__(self):
        return f'{self.first_name} {self.last_name}'
```

Run Migrations: Create the necessary database tables by running the migrations:
bash
Copy
python manage.py makemigrations
python manage.py migrate

Create Views and URL Routing: In users/views.py, define the views to handle the CRUD operations:
python
Copy

```python
from django.http import JsonResponse
from django.views.decorators.csrf import csrf_exempt
from users.models import User
from django.views.decorators.http import require_http_methods
import json

@csrf_exempt
@require_http_methods(["POST"])
def create_user(request):
    data = json.loads(request.body)
    user = User.objects.create(
        first_name=data['first_name'],
        last_name=data['last_name'],
        email=data['email']
    )
    return JsonResponse({'message': 'User created', 'id': user.id}, status=201)

@require_http_methods(["GET"])
def get_users(request):
    users = User.objects.all()
    return JsonResponse(list(users.values()), safe=False)

@require_http_methods(["GET"])
def get_user(request, id):
    user = User.objects.get(id=id)
    return JsonResponse({'id': user.id, 'first_name': user.first_name, 'last_name':
user.last_name, 'email': user.email})
```

56

```python
@csrf_exempt
@require_http_methods(["PUT"])
def update_user(request, id):
    data = json.loads(request.body)
    user = User.objects.get(id=id)
    user.first_name = data['first_name']
    user.last_name = data['last_name']
    user.email = data['email']
    user.save()
    return JsonResponse({'message': 'User updated'})


@csrf_exempt
@require_http_methods(["DELETE"])
def delete_user(request, id):
    user = User.objects.get(id=id)
    user.delete()
    return JsonResponse({'message': 'User deleted'})
```

Define URL Routing: In users/urls.py, add URL routing to map the views to specific endpoints:
python
Copy
```python
from django.urls import path
from . import views

urlpatterns = [
    path('users/', views.get_users),
    path('users/<int:id>/', views.get_user),
    path('users/create/', views.create_user),
    path('users/update/<int:id>/', views.update_user),
    path('users/delete/<int:id>/', views.delete_user),
]
```
Finally, include these URLs in the main project's urls.py:
python
Copy
```python
from django.contrib import admin
from django.urls import path, include
```

```
urlpatterns = [
    path('admin/', admin.site.urls),
    path('api/', include('users.urls')),
]
```

Run the Django Application: Start the Django development server:
bash
Copy
python manage.py runserver

Your API will now be available at **http://localhost:8000/api/users/** and can perform CRUD operations with PostgreSQL.

5.2 Creating RESTful Endpoints for PostgreSQL

In this section, we will go deeper into creating the RESTful API endpoints for the CRUD operations on PostgreSQL data. The endpoints will allow you to handle **Create**, **Read**, **Update**, and **Delete** operations through a RESTful interface.

5.2.1 RESTful API Design Principles

A RESTful API follows certain principles, which include:

- **Statelessness**: Every request from the client to the server must contain all the information necessary to understand and process the request.
- **Resource-Based**: Each endpoint represents a resource, which is typically a noun, such as /users, /products, etc.
- **HTTP Methods**: Use HTTP methods (GET, POST, PUT, DELETE) to represent operations on resources.

In our example, we will create endpoints to handle users, with the following operations:

- **POST /users**: Create a new user.
- **GET /users**: Retrieve all users.
- **GET /users/{id}**: Retrieve a specific user.
- **PUT /users/{id}**: Update a specific user.
- **DELETE /users/{id}**: Delete a specific user.

5.2.2 Create Endpoint

The **Create** operation adds a new user to the PostgreSQL database.

python
Copy
```
@csrf_exempt
@require_http_methods(["POST"])
def create_user(request):
    data = json.loads(request.body)
    user = User.objects.create(
        first_name=data['first_name'],
        last_name=data['last_name'],
        email=data['email']
    )
    return JsonResponse({'message': 'User created', 'id': user.id}, status=201)
```

5.2.3 Read Endpoint

The **Read** operation retrieves users from the database.

python
Copy
```
@require_http_methods(["GET"])
def get_users(request):
    users = User.objects.all()
    return JsonResponse(list(users.values()), safe=False)
```

5.2.4 Update Endpoint

The **Update** operation modifies an existing user.

python
Copy
```
@csrf_exempt
@require_http_methods(["PUT"])
def update_user(request, id):
    data = json.loads(request.body)
    user = User.objects.get(id=id)
```

59

```python
user.first_name = data['first_name']
user.last_name = data['last_name']
user.email = data['email']
user.save()
return JsonResponse({'message': 'User updated'})
```

5.2.5 Delete Endpoint

The **Delete** operation removes a user from the database.

python
Copy
```python
@csrf_exempt
@require_http_methods(["DELETE"])
def delete_user(request, id):
    user = User.objects.get(id=id)
    user.delete()
    return JsonResponse({'message': 'User deleted'})
```

5.3 Managing Database Transactions

In a database-driven application, managing transactions is crucial to ensure data consistency, prevent data corruption, and provide reliable error handling. PostgreSQL, like most relational databases, supports **ACID** transactions, ensuring that operations are **Atomic**, **Consistent**, **Isolated**, and **Durable**. When building a RESTful API, handling transactions properly is essential to maintaining data integrity, especially when multiple operations are involved.

5.3.1 What Are Database Transactions?

A **database transaction** is a sequence of one or more database operations (like insert, update, delete, or select) that are treated as a single unit of work. If any part of the transaction fails, the entire transaction is rolled back, ensuring that the database remains in a consistent state.

In PostgreSQL, you can group several SQL commands into a single transaction, and if any command fails, you can **rollback** the entire transaction to its original state.

5.3.2 Using Transactions in Django

Django's ORM automatically wraps database operations in transactions, but you can also manage transactions manually using the atomic block. This is useful when you need more control over how multiple queries are executed together.

Example: Using atomic for Manual Transaction Management

python
Copy

```python
from django.db import transaction

def create_user_and_order(user_data, order_data):
    try:
        with transaction.atomic():
            # Creating a new user
            user = User.objects.create(
                first_name=user_data['first_name'],
                last_name=user_data['last_name'],
                email=user_data['email']
            )

            # Creating an order for the user
            order = Order.objects.create(
                user=user,
                product_name=order_data['product_name'],
                amount=order_data['amount']
            )

            return user, order

    except Exception as e:
        # In case of error, all changes are rolled back
        print(f"Error occurred: {str(e)}")
        return None, None
```

In this example, both user creation and order creation are wrapped in a transaction.atomic() block. If any exception is raised within this block, both the user and the order will not be saved to the database, and the transaction will be rolled back.

61

5.3.3 Using Transactions in Flask with SQLAlchemy

In Flask, if you're using SQLAlchemy as the ORM, transactions can be managed using session.commit() and session.rollback(). SQLAlchemy handles transactions automatically, but you can use explicit transaction handling when necessary.

Example: Using Explicit Transaction Handling in Flask
python
Copy

```python
from flask import Flask, request, jsonify
from flask_sqlalchemy import SQLAlchemy
from sqlalchemy.exc import SQLAlchemyError

app = Flask(__name__)
app.config['SQLALCHEMY_DATABASE_URI'] =
'postgresql://username:password@localhost/mydb'
app.config['SQLALCHEMY_TRACK_MODIFICATIONS'] = False
db = SQLAlchemy(app)

class User(db.Model):
    id = db.Column(db.Integer, primary_key=True)
    first_name = db.Column(db.String(100))
    last_name = db.Column(db.String(100))
    email = db.Column(db.String(100), unique=True)

@app.route('/create', methods=['POST'])
def create_user():
    data = request.get_json()

    try:
        # Start a transaction
        db.session.begin()

        new_user = User(first_name=data['first_name'], last_name=data['last_name'],
email=data['email'])
        db.session.add(new_user)

        # Commit the transaction
        db.session.commit()
```

```
    return jsonify({'message': 'User created successfully'}), 201
except SQLAlchemyError as e:
    # Rollback in case of error
    db.session.rollback()
    return jsonify({'error': str(e)}), 500
finally:
    # Always close the session
    db.session.remove()

if __name__ == '__main__':
    app.run(debug=True)
```

In this Flask example, we manually begin a transaction using db.session.begin(), commit it with db.session.commit(), and handle any exceptions by rolling back the session with db.session.rollback().

5.3.4 Transaction Isolation Levels

PostgreSQL supports multiple **transaction isolation levels** that control the visibility of uncommitted data. The four main isolation levels are:

1. **Read Uncommitted**: Allows reading data that is in the process of being changed by another transaction. This is the least strict and can lead to **dirty reads**.
2. **Read Committed**: Ensures that no dirty reads occur, but it still allows **non-repeatable reads**, where the data you read might change during the course of your transaction.
3. **Repeatable Read**: Guarantees that data read within a transaction remains consistent throughout the transaction. However, **phantom reads** can still occur, meaning that new rows can be inserted by other transactions.
4. **Serializable**: Provides the strictest level of isolation. Transactions are executed as though they were serial, with no other transactions allowed to interfere.

In Django, you can set the isolation level using the transaction.atomic() context manager, but PostgreSQL's default is usually sufficient for most use cases.

5.4 Implementing Data Validation

Data validation is a critical step in building a reliable API, ensuring that the data entered into the system is both accurate and consistent. Without validation, users might input

63

incorrect, incomplete, or malicious data that can compromise the integrity of your system.

5.4.1 Why Data Validation is Important

Validating input data is essential for:

- **Preventing SQL Injection**: Ensuring that user inputs do not contain harmful SQL code that can be executed on the database.
- **Ensuring Data Integrity**: Preventing invalid data types or missing required fields that could break the application logic.
- **Improving User Experience**: Providing clear feedback when incorrect or incomplete data is entered.

5.4.2 Implementing Validation in Django

In Django, validation is typically done at the model level using **ModelForm** or within the views using **Django's forms module**.

Model Validation Example in Django

python
Copy
```
from django.db import models
from django.core.exceptions import ValidationError

class User(models.Model):
    first_name = models.CharField(max_length=100)
    last_name = models.CharField(max_length=100)
    email = models.EmailField(unique=True)

    def clean(self):
        if not self.first_name or not self.last_name:
            raise ValidationError("First name and last name are required.")
        if len(self.first_name) < 2:
            raise ValidationError("First name should be at least 2 characters.")
```

In this example, the clean method is overridden to implement custom validation logic for the User model. It ensures that the first_name and last_name are not empty and enforces a length requirement for first_name.

64

Using Django Forms for Validation

Django provides built-in form validation that automatically handles fields and errors. For example:

```python
Copy
from django import forms

class UserForm(forms.Form):
    first_name = forms.CharField(min_length=2, max_length=100)
    last_name = forms.CharField(min_length=2, max_length=100)
    email = forms.EmailField()

    def clean_email(self):
        email = self.cleaned_data.get('email')
        if User.objects.filter(email=email).exists():
            raise forms.ValidationError("Email already exists.")
        return email
```

In this UserForm, custom validation ensures that the email provided does not already exist in the User table.

5.4.3 Implementing Validation in Flask with WTForms

Flask integrates with the **WTForms** library for handling form data and validation. WTForms allows you to define forms and perform validation.

Example of WTForms Validation in Flask

```python
Copy
from flask import Flask, request, jsonify
from wtforms import Form, StringField, EmailField
from wtforms.validators import InputRequired, Length, Email

app = Flask(__name__)

class UserForm(Form):
    first_name = StringField('First Name', [InputRequired(), Length(min=2, max=100)])
```

```
last_name = StringField('Last Name', [InputRequired(), Length(min=2, max=100)])
email = EmailField('Email', [InputRequired(), Email()])

@app.route('/users', methods=['POST'])
def create_user():
    form = UserForm(request.form)
    if form.validate():
        # Process the valid data
        return jsonify({'message': 'User created successfully'}), 201
    else:
        return jsonify({'errors': form.errors}), 400
```

This example uses **WTForms** to validate the first_name, last_name, and email fields, ensuring that they meet the required constraints.

5.5 Error Handling and Logging in PostgreSQL APIs

Effective error handling and logging are essential to any production system, especially for APIs that interact with a relational database like PostgreSQL. Proper error handling ensures that your application can gracefully manage unexpected issues, while logging helps you track and debug errors when they occur.

5.5.1 Common PostgreSQL Errors

When working with PostgreSQL, several common errors can occur, such as:

- **Unique Constraint Violation**: Occurs when attempting to insert duplicate data where a unique constraint (e.g., on a primary key or unique column) is violated.
- **Foreign Key Constraint Violation**: Occurs when trying to insert or update data that violates a foreign key relationship, typically when trying to reference a non-existent record.
- **Null Value Violation**: Occurs when attempting to insert a NULL value into a column that does not allow it.

5.5.2 Implementing Error Handling in Django

In Django, error handling is done at both the database and view levels. The try-except block is used for handling database-related exceptions.

66

Django Error Handling Example

python
Copy

```python
from django.db import IntegrityError

def create_user(request):
    try:
        user = User.objects.create(first_name=request.data['first_name'],
                        last_name=request.data['last_name'],
                        email=request.data['email'])
        return JsonResponse({'message': 'User created successfully'}, status=201)
    except IntegrityError as e:
        return JsonResponse({'error': str(e)}, status=400)
```

In this example, an IntegrityError is caught if there is a constraint violation, and a proper response is sent back to the client.

5.5.3 Logging API Operations

Logging provides invaluable insights into application behavior, helping developers debug issues and track usage patterns. You can use Python's built-in logging library to log events in your application.

Setting Up Logging in Flask

python
Copy

```python
import logging

# Configure logging
logging.basicConfig(level=logging.INFO, format='%(asctime)s - %(message)s')

@app.route('/create', methods=['POST'])
def create_user():
    try:
        user = User.create(first_name="John", last_name="Doe",
email="john.doe@example.com")
        logging.info("User created successfully: %s", user.email)
        return jsonify({"message": "User created"}), 201
    except Exception as e:
```

67

```
logging.error("Error creating user: %s", str(e))
return jsonify({"error": "Error occurred"}), 500
```

This logging setup in Flask records both successful user creations and errors, which can then be stored in log files or forwarded to external monitoring services like **CloudWatch**.

5.5.4 Using Cloud Logging (AWS CloudWatch)

For production-level applications, using a cloud-based logging solution like **AWS CloudWatch** allows you to capture logs and monitor API activity in real time. By configuring **CloudWatch Logs**, you can easily track API requests, database queries, and errors to gain insights into your system's performance and health.

Chapter 6: Advanced RESTful API Design Best Practices

6.1 API Authentication and Authorization

One of the core principles of modern API design is ensuring that only authorized users can access sensitive resources. As web applications grow, managing access control becomes increasingly critical. **API Authentication** and **Authorization** are two essential mechanisms that help protect your APIs from unauthorized access while ensuring that legitimate users can interact with your services as intended.

6.1.1 What Is API Authentication?

Authentication refers to the process of verifying the identity of a user or system trying to access an API. It is essentially asking: *Who are you?*

Authentication is typically handled using one of the following methods:

API Keys: A unique key provided by the server that identifies a client or application. It's a simple, but less secure method of authentication. API keys are often sent in the header of requests, for example:
bash
Copy
```
GET /user/data HTTP/1.1
Host: api.example.com
Authorization: ApiKey your-api-key-here
```

- **Basic Authentication**: A method where the client sends a username and password as a base64-encoded string in the Authorization header. Although simple, it's often considered insecure because the credentials are exposed if the connection isn't encrypted via HTTPS.
  bash
  Copy
  ```
  GET /user/data HTTP/1.1
  ```

```
Host: api.example.com
Authorization: Basic base64encoded-username:password
```

- **Bearer Tokens**: In this case, the server authenticates the user and issues a token that is sent with subsequent requests. This is often used with OAuth and JWT (JSON Web Tokens), which are more secure than basic authentication.
  bash
  Copy
  GET /user/data HTTP/1.1

Host: api.example.com
Authorization: Bearer your-jwt-token-here

6.1.2 What Is API Authorization?

While **authentication** answers the question of "Who are you?", **authorization** determines what actions a user or application can perform after they are authenticated. In simpler terms, authorization is about *what you are allowed to do*. This includes defining access control policies for resources based on user roles or permissions.

Authorization methods include:

Role-Based Access Control (RBAC): With RBAC, users are assigned roles (e.g., **admin**, **editor**, **viewer**) and access to resources is based on these roles. For example, an **admin** may have access to all resources, while a **viewer** may only have access to read-only resources.
Example:
json
Copy
```
{
  "user": "john_doe",
  "role": "admin"
}
```

- **Attribute-Based Access Control (ABAC)**: ABAC provides more fine-grained access control by evaluating attributes of the user, the resource, and the environment. For instance, a user may only access a resource if they belong to a particular department or group.
  Example:
  json
  Copy
```
{
  "user": "john_doe",
```

70

```
"department": "finance",
"resource": "salary_info"
}
```

- **OAuth Scopes**: OAuth allows developers to set **scopes**, which define specific actions or resources the user can access. A scope might be a read, write, or delete permission on specific resources.
  Example:
  json
  Copy

```
{
"user": "john_doe",
"scopes": ["read:user_data", "write:posts"]
}
```

6.1.3 Best Practices for Authentication and Authorization

- **Use HTTPS for All API Calls**: Regardless of the authentication method, always enforce **HTTPS** to prevent credentials and tokens from being intercepted in transit.
- **Token Expiry**: Always set expiration times for authentication tokens. This reduces the risk of a compromised token being used indefinitely. Implement token refresh mechanisms as needed.
- **Use Least Privilege**: Implement the principle of least privilege, granting users only the permissions they absolutely need to perform their tasks.
- **Centralized Authentication**: Use centralized authentication mechanisms, such as **Identity and Access Management (IAM)** services like **AWS Cognito**, **Auth0, or OAuth2 providers** to handle user authentication and authorization in a secure and scalable way.
- **Avoid Storing Sensitive Information**: Do not store sensitive authentication details (like passwords) in plain text. Use **bcrypt, argon2**, or similar hashing algorithms to securely store passwords.

6.2 Implementing JWT and OAuth2

JSON Web Tokens (JWT) and **OAuth2** are widely used techniques for implementing secure API authentication and authorization. Both technologies help ensure that sensitive data is securely shared between services, while maintaining scalability and flexibility.

6.2.1 What is JWT (JSON Web Token)?

JWT is an open standard (RFC 7519) that defines a compact and self-contained method for securely transmitting information between parties as a JSON object. JWTs are used extensively for authentication and authorization in modern web applications.

A **JWT** typically consists of three parts:

Header: Contains the type of token (JWT) and the signing algorithm (e.g., HMAC SHA256 or RSA).
Example:
json
Copy

```
{
  "alg": "HS256",
  "typ": "JWT"
}
```

Payload: Contains the claims (the data). Claims are statements about an entity (typically, the user) and additional data. For instance, a claim could be the user's ID, roles, or expiration time of the token. Claims can be public (standard claims like iss, exp, sub) or private (application-specific data).
Example:
json
Copy

```
{
  "sub": "1234567890",
  "name": "John Doe",
  "iat": 1516239022
}
```

Signature: To create the signature part you take the encoded header, encoded payload, a secret, and the algorithm specified in the header. The signature is used to verify that the sender of the JWT is who it says it is, and to ensure the message wasn't tampered with.

72

Example:

scss

Copy

```
HMACSHA256(
    base64UrlEncode(header) + "." +
    base64UrlEncode(payload),
    secret)
```

The resulting token looks like:

css

Copy

```
header.payload.signature
```

JWTs are widely used for **stateless authentication** in RESTful APIs because they allow the server to authenticate requests without needing to maintain session state.

JWT Authentication Example

User Login (Authentication): When the user logs in, the server validates the user's credentials and returns a JWT containing claims about the user (e.g., userID, role, exp for expiration).

Example response:

json

Copy

```
{
    "token":
"eyJhbGciOiJIUzI1NiIsInR5cCI6IkpXVCJ9.eyJzdWIiOiIxMjM0NTY3ODkwIiwibmFt
ZSI6IkpvaG4gRG9lIiwiaWF0IjoxNTE2MjM5MDIyfQ.SflKxwRJSMeKKF2QT4fwpM
eJf36POk6yJV_adQssw5c"
}
```

73

API Request with JWT: For subsequent requests, the client sends the JWT in the Authorization header as a **Bearer token**.
Example:
bash
Copy
GET /protected-resource
Authorization: Bearer <jwt_token>

1. The server verifies the JWT using the secret key or public key (if using RSA) and grants access to the requested resource if the token is valid.
2. **Token Expiration and Refresh**: JWT tokens should have an expiration time (exp claim). When the token expires, users must authenticate again, or they can use a **refresh token** to obtain a new JWT without re-authenticating.

6.2.2 What is OAuth2?

OAuth2 (Open Authorization 2.0) is an authorization framework that allows third-party applications to access a user's resources without exposing their credentials. OAuth2 is widely used for **delegated access**—for example, when a user logs into an app using their **Google** or **Facebook** credentials.

OAuth2 works with **authorization tokens**, which are issued by an authorization server and used by the client application to access protected resources.

OAuth2 Workflow

OAuth2 typically uses four roles:

1. **Resource Owner**: The user who owns the data (e.g., a Google account holder).
2. **Client**: The application that wants to access the user's data (e.g., a third-party app that needs access to the user's Google Calendar).
3. **Authorization Server**: The server that authenticates the user and issues access tokens (e.g., Google's OAuth2 server).
4. **Resource Server**: The server that hosts the protected resources (e.g., Google Calendar API).

OAuth2 Grant Types

OAuth2 defines several **grant types**, each serving different use cases:

- **Authorization Code**: This is the most secure flow. It is used when the client is a web server. The client first redirects the user to the authorization server for authentication. The authorization server then redirects the user back to the client with an authorization code, which the client can exchange for an access token.
- **Implicit**: Used in client-side applications (e.g., single-page apps). It returns the access token directly without the need for an intermediate authorization code.
- **Client Credentials**: Used by clients to authenticate themselves when accessing their own resources, rather than on behalf of a user.
- **Password Credentials**: In this flow, the user provides their username and password to the client, which is then used to request an access token from the authorization server.

OAuth2 Example with Authorization Code Flow

User Authorization: The client redirects the user to the authorization server (e.g., Google) to log in and grant permission.
Example:
bash
Copy
```
GET
/authorize?response_type=code&client_id=your-client-id&redirect_uri=http://localhost/
callback
```

Authorization Code: After the user grants permission, the authorization server redirects them back to the client with an authorization code.
Example:
bash
Copy
```
GET /callback?code=authorization_code
```

Access Token Request: The client exchanges the authorization code for an access token.
Example request:
makefile
Copy

```
POST /token
Content-Type: application/x-www-form-urlencoded
client_id=your-client-id
client_secret=your-client-secret
code=authorization_code
redirect_uri=http://localhost/callback
```

Access Resource: The client uses the access token to request protected resources from the resource server.
Example request:
sql
Copy

```
GET /user/profile
Authorization: Bearer access_token
```

6.3 API Versioning Strategies

API versioning is a crucial aspect of API design that ensures backward compatibility as the API evolves over time. As applications grow, new features are added, and existing features may be deprecated or changed. Without versioning, existing users may experience breaking changes when the API is updated, leading to a poor user experience. Proper API versioning allows developers to make changes to the API while ensuring that existing clients continue to function.

6.3.1 Why API Versioning is Important

Versioning ensures that clients using older versions of the API can continue working even after new changes have been made to the API. It also allows for smoother transitions when deprecating old features or introducing new functionality. Without versioning, updates could cause disruptions in services, requiring all clients to adapt immediately to the new changes.

76

6.3.2 Common API Versioning Strategies

URI Path Versioning (Most Common): This is the most common and straightforward approach. The API version is included in the URL path, making it easy for clients to specify which version of the API they are using.
Example:
bash
Copy

```
GET /v1/users
GET /v2/users
```

1. **Pros**:
   - Easy to implement and understand.
   - Clear separation between versions.
2. **Cons**:
   - As the number of versions increases, the URL structure becomes less clean.

Query Parameter Versioning: In this strategy, the version is included as a query parameter in the API request. It allows the client to specify the version without changing the URL structure.
Example:
pgsql
Copy

```
GET /users?version=1
GET /users?version=2
```

3. **Pros**:
   - Keeps the URL structure clean.
   - Easy to implement.
4. **Cons**:
   - May not be as visible or intuitive as path versioning.

Custom Header Versioning: API versioning can also be done through custom HTTP headers. Clients specify the version of the API they want to use in the Accept header or a custom header, such as X-API-Version.
Example:
bash
Copy

```
GET /users
Accept: application/vnd.myapi.v1+json
```

5. **Pros**:
    - Clean URLs, no need for version information in the URL or query parameters.
    - Versioning information is separated from the resource path, making the URL more focused.
6. **Cons**:
    - Slightly less intuitive for clients, as versioning is hidden in headers.
    - Requires more configuration and support in the API.

Accept Header Versioning (Content Negotiation): In this method, API versions are specified via the Accept header using content negotiation. The client includes the version information in the Accept header.
Example:
bash
Copy
GET /users
Accept: application/vnd.myapi.v1+json

7. **Pros**:
    - No changes to the URL structure.
    - Ideal for APIs that need to support multiple formats (JSON, XML, etc.).
8. **Cons**:
    - More complex than path versioning.
    - Requires careful management of content types and headers.

6.3.3 Best Practices for API Versioning

- **Start with clear versioning policies**: Ensure that versioning is implemented early in the development of your API, making it easier to manage changes as your API evolves.
- **Maintain backward compatibility**: Whenever possible, avoid breaking changes in newer versions of the API. Deprecate features rather than removing them entirely.
- **Use semantic versioning**: If using path versioning or query parameters, ensure that your versioning system follows a logical format, such as **v1**, **v2**, etc., or even **v1.1**, **v1.2** for minor changes.
- **Deprecate gracefully**: When removing or changing functionality, provide clients with sufficient notice and support migration to the newer version.

6.4 Swagger/OpenAPI Documentation Generation

78

One of the most important aspects of building a RESTful API is ensuring that it is well-documented. Proper documentation helps developers understand how to interact with your API, the expected inputs, and the possible responses. Tools like **Swagger** and **OpenAPI** provide an automatic way to generate documentation based on the API's structure, making it easier for clients and developers to integrate and use the API.

6.4.1 What is Swagger and OpenAPI?

Swagger is a framework for designing, building, and documenting RESTful APIs. It is now part of the **OpenAPI Specification (OAS)**, a standard for describing APIs that is used by many API tools and services.

- **Swagger** refers to both the tools and the specification itself.
- **OpenAPI** is the name of the specification used to define the API structure, and Swagger is one of the tools that helps generate OpenAPI-compliant documentation.

Swagger provides a **UI** for visualizing the API and **JSON or YAML**-based specifications that describe the API's endpoints, parameters, responses, and other details.

6.4.2 Why Use Swagger/OpenAPI for API Documentation?

- **Interactive Documentation**: Swagger provides an interactive UI that allows users to test API endpoints directly from the documentation. This is an incredibly useful feature for API developers and clients.
- **Automatic Documentation Generation**: Tools like **Swagger UI** can automatically generate interactive documentation from your API code or OpenAPI specification, keeping the documentation up-to-date with the latest changes in your API.
- **Standardization**: OpenAPI provides a standardized way of describing API endpoints, parameters, and responses, making it easier for developers to understand how to interact with your API.

6.4.3 Generating API Documentation with Swagger/OpenAPI

Swagger/OpenAPI provides various tools to generate API documentation based on annotations in your code or configuration files. Below are some of the ways to integrate Swagger with your API.

1. Using Swagger with Flask

Flask integrates with Swagger using libraries such as **Flask-RESTPlus** or **Flask-Swagger-UI** to auto-generate OpenAPI-compliant documentation. Below is an example using **Flask-RESTPlus**:

Install Flask-RESTPlus:
bash
Copy
```
pip install flask-restplus
```

Create a Flask App with Swagger:
python
Copy
```
from flask import Flask
from flask_restplus import Api, Resource

app = Flask(__name__)
api = Api(app)

@api.route('/users')
class UserList(Resource):
    def get(self):
        return {'message': 'List of users'}

if __name__ == '__main__':
    app.run(debug=True)
```

With this setup, Flask-RESTPlus automatically generates Swagger-based API documentation that you can access at /swagger-ui/ on your Flask server.

2. Using Swagger with Django

Django integrates with **drf-yasg** (Yet Another Swagger Generator) to auto-generate Swagger UI documentation for Django REST Framework APIs.

Install drf-yasg:
bash
Copy
```
pip install drf-yasg
```

Configure Swagger with Django: In your Django urls.py, include the Swagger schema view:
python
Copy
```
from rest_framework import routers
from drf_yasg.views import get_schema_view
from drf_yasg import openapi
from django.urls import path, include

schema_view = get_schema_view(
    openapi.Info(
        title="My API",
        default_version='v1',
        description="Test description",
        terms_of_service="https://www.google.com/policies/terms/",
        contact=openapi.Contact(email="contact@myapi.local"),
        license=openapi.License(name="BSD License"),
    ),
    public=True,
)

urlpatterns = [
    path('admin/', admin.site.urls),
    path('api/', include('myapp.urls')),
    path('swagger/', schema_view.with_ui('swagger', cache_timeout=0)),
]
```

Access Swagger Documentation: After running the server, the Swagger documentation will be available at **/swagger/**. You'll get an interactive UI where you can explore and test the API endpoints.

6.5 Caching and Rate Limiting for Performance

As APIs grow and handle more traffic, **caching** and **rate limiting** become essential techniques for improving performance and ensuring a smooth user experience. Caching speeds up the response time by storing frequently accessed data, while rate limiting helps control the number of requests a client can make to prevent overloading the server.

6.5.1 Caching

Caching is the process of storing copies of expensive or frequently requested data in a fast-access storage medium. When a client requests data that has been cached, the response is returned from the cache rather than querying the database again, significantly reducing response times.

Types of Caching

In-Memory Caching: This stores cached data in the server's memory. Examples include **Memcached** and **Redis**.

  - **Redis** is particularly popular due to its fast in-memory data structure store, which supports strings, hashes, lists, sets, and more.

HTTP Caching: HTTP headers like Cache-Control, ETag, and Expires can be used to instruct clients and intermediate servers to cache API responses.
Example:
python
Copy

```
@app.route('/users')
@cache.cached(timeout=60)  # Cache for 60 seconds
def get_users():
    return jsonify(users)
```

Database Caching: Some database systems (like PostgreSQL) support caching at the query level, which can improve performance for frequently executed queries.

82

Best Practices for Caching

- **Use caching for expensive queries**: Cache results from frequent, expensive queries (e.g., database joins or API calls to external services).
- **Cache with an expiry time**: Set cache expiry times to avoid serving stale data.
- **Invalidate cache when data changes**: Ensure that your cache is updated when the underlying data changes, either through time-based expiry or through manual invalidation.

6.5.2 Rate Limiting

Rate limiting controls the number of API requests a client can make within a specific time window. It helps protect your API from abuse and ensures that all users have fair access to the server resources.

Types of Rate Limiting

1. **Fixed Window Rate Limiting**: Limits requests within fixed time intervals (e.g., 100 requests per minute).
2. **Sliding Window Rate Limiting**: Provides a more flexible approach, where the limit is based on a rolling window (e.g., 100 requests in the past 60 seconds).
3. **Leaky Bucket**: Uses a bucket where requests are added; if the bucket is full, further requests are discarded.
4. **Token Bucket**: Tokens are added to a bucket at a fixed rate. Clients can use tokens for requests, and if there are no tokens, the request is denied.

Implementing Rate Limiting in Flask

To implement rate limiting in Flask, you can use extensions like **Flask-Limiter**:

Install Flask-Limiter:
bash
Copy
```
pip install Flask-Limiter
```

Set Up Rate Limiting:
python
Copy
```
from flask import Flask
from flask_limiter import Limiter

app = Flask(__name__)
limiter = Limiter(app, key_func=lambda: request.remote_addr)

@app.route('/users')
@limiter.limit("10 per minute")  # Limit to 10 requests per minute
def get_users():
    return jsonify(users)
```

Best Practices for Rate Limiting

- **Customize the limits based on user roles**: For example, authenticated users may have a higher rate limit than anonymous users.
- **Provide feedback when the limit is exceeded**: Return a clear HTTP response code like **429 Too Many Requests** when the limit is exceeded, along with information on when the user can try again.
- **Monitor and adjust rate limits**: Keep track of your usage patterns and adjust rate limits to prevent abuse without restricting legitimate users.

Chapter 7: Optimizing DynamoDB for High Performance

7.1 Understanding Partitions and Keys

Amazon DynamoDB is a fully managed NoSQL database service designed to handle high-velocity workloads. The way DynamoDB structures and accesses data is key to its scalability and performance. One of the most important concepts in DynamoDB is the **partitioning** mechanism, which directly impacts how efficiently data can be accessed and stored. In this section, we will explore the concept of **partitions, partition keys**, and **sort keys**, which are crucial for optimizing your DynamoDB performance.

7.1.1 DynamoDB Data Model: Partitions and Keys

DynamoDB stores data in tables, and each table is divided into multiple **partitions**. Each partition contains a set of data, and the data within each partition is determined by a combination of the table's **primary key** and the **partition key**.

Primary Key in DynamoDB

In DynamoDB, each item (or row) in a table is uniquely identified by a **primary key**. The primary key consists of one or two components:

1. **Partition Key (also known as Hash Key)**: The partition key is a single attribute that DynamoDB uses to determine which partition an item will be placed in. DynamoDB uses an internal hash function to map the partition key value to a partition. Items with the same partition key are stored together in the same partition, which ensures that they can be retrieved quickly.
   Example: In a Users table, you might choose userID as the partition key. All data related to a specific user (such as profile details, orders, etc.) will be grouped together based on this partition key.
2. **Sort Key (also known as Range Key)**: The sort key allows for more fine-grained control of how data is organized within each partition. With the addition of a sort key, you can store multiple items with the same partition key but distinguish them based on the sort key value. This enables you to model one-to-many relationships and perform queries based on both the partition key and sort key.
   Example: In a Posts table, the userID could be the partition key, and the

postDate could be the sort key. This allows you to store all posts from a particular user in the same partition, but differentiate them by the post date.

How DynamoDB Uses Partitions

DynamoDB automatically distributes the data across multiple partitions as your table grows. The partition key plays a critical role in this distribution. Here's how it works:

1. **Hashing the Partition Key**: DynamoDB uses a **hashing algorithm** to map the partition key to a partition. The more evenly your partition key values are distributed, the better DynamoDB can distribute the data across partitions. This minimizes the risk of **hot partitions**, which occur when too much data is stored in a single partition.
2. **Range of Partition Keys**: When you choose a partition key, it's essential to pick one that has a wide range of values. If your partition key is highly skewed or only has a small set of possible values (e.g., userID = 1), your data could end up concentrated in a single partition, leading to uneven performance.
3. **Scaling**: As your table grows, DynamoDB automatically adds new partitions to accommodate the increasing load. This automatic scaling is one of the reasons DynamoDB can handle high-performance workloads seamlessly.

Example of a Partition Key and Sort Key Table Design

Here's an example of a table where we use the userID as the partition key and timestamp as the sort key:

- **Table Name**: UserActivities
- **Partition Key**: userID
- **Sort Key**: timestamp

Sample Data:

userID	timestamp	activity
101	1622530800	Login
101	1622531400	View Product
102	1622532000	Logout
103	1622532200	Sign Up
101	1622533000	Purchase

In this table, all activities by a user are stored in the same partition. The sort key allows DynamoDB to efficiently retrieve activities by timestamp for each user.

7.1.2 How to Optimize Partitions for High Performance

1. **Choose a High-Cardinality Partition Key**: A partition key with many unique values will help distribute your data evenly across multiple partitions. This improves the overall performance of read and write operations.
   Example: Instead of using city as a partition key for a Users table (which might have a small set of possible values), consider using userID, which has a much larger set of possible values.

2. **Avoid Hot Partitions**: A **hot partition** occurs when too many items are mapped to a single partition due to a skewed partition key. This can slow down read and write operations and cause throttling. To avoid hot partitions, choose partition keys with evenly distributed values.
   Example: Avoid using timestamps as partition keys (e.g., year, month), as they tend to be less evenly distributed and could create hot partitions for frequently accessed time periods.

3. **Monitor and Adjust**: Use AWS CloudWatch to monitor the throughput and latency of your DynamoDB tables. If you see signs of hot partitions, consider restructuring your partition keys or using **Global Secondary Indexes (GSI)** or **Local Secondary Indexes (LSI)** to improve query performance.

7.2 Choosing the Right Indexes (Global Secondary Indexes and Local Secondary Indexes)

Indexes in DynamoDB play a significant role in optimizing query performance by allowing you to retrieve data efficiently based on attributes other than the partition key and sort key. DynamoDB supports two types of indexes: **Global Secondary Indexes (GSI)** and **Local Secondary Indexes (LSI)**. Understanding when and how to use these indexes is critical for achieving high performance in DynamoDB.

7.2.1 What is a Global Secondary Index (GSI)?

A **Global Secondary Index (GSI)** allows you to create an index on any attribute in your table, not just the partition key or sort key. A GSI enables fast queries on non-primary key attributes while still maintaining DynamoDB's scalability.

Key Features of GSIs:

- **Global**: GSIs can be created on any attribute, including those that are not part of the primary key. You can query any attribute using the partition and sort keys that are different from the base table's primary key.
- **Separate Throughput**: GSIs have their own throughput settings, separate from the base table. This allows you to allocate more resources to indexes that are frequently queried, improving performance.
- **Eventually Consistent**: GSI queries are **eventually consistent** by default, meaning there may be a slight delay before the indexed data is updated.

When to Use GSIs

- **Need to Query by Non-Primary Key Attributes**: If you frequently query data based on attributes that are not part of the partition or sort key, a GSI can significantly improve query performance.
- **Access Patterns**: If you need to support multiple access patterns, such as querying by multiple attributes, GSIs provide a flexible way to index those fields.

Example of Using a GSI

Consider a Products table where the primary key is productID (partition key), but you also want to query products based on category (a non-primary key attribute). You can create a GSI with category as the partition key and price as the sort key.

- **Table Name**: Products
- **Primary Key**: productID
- **GSI**: category (partition key), price (sort key)

With this GSI, you can quickly query all products in a specific category sorted by price.

7.2.2 What is a Local Secondary Index (LSI)?

A **Local Secondary Index (LSI)** is similar to a GSI, but it's bound to the same partition key as the base table. LSI allows you to create alternative sort keys while keeping the same partition key, making it ideal for queries that need to retrieve items in different sorted orders without changing the partition key.

Key Features of LSIs:

- **Local**: LSIs are tied to the partition key of the base table. This means that each partition has its own local index.
- **Same Partition Key**: You can query your data using a different sort key, but the partition key remains the same as the base table.
- **Indexed on Sort Key**: LSIs only change the way the data is sorted, not the partition key. You can only create up to **5 LSIs per table**.

When to Use LSIs

- **Different Sort Order**: LSIs are ideal when you need to access data in multiple different sort orders. For example, if you have a table of blog posts with postID as the partition key and date as the sort key, you might create an LSI with views as the sort key to sort the posts by view count.
- **Small to Medium-Sized Datasets**: LSIs are best used for smaller datasets where you need to maintain strict control over data access patterns within each partition.

Example of Using an LSI

Consider an Orders table where the partition key is customerID and the sort key is orderDate. If you wanted to also query orders by orderStatus (e.g., pending, shipped, delivered), you could create an LSI with orderStatus as the sort key.

- **Table Name**: Orders
- **Primary Key**: customerID, orderDate
- **LSI**: customerID (partition key), orderStatus (sort key)

With this setup, you can efficiently query orders by orderStatus for each customer.

7.2.3 Choosing Between GSIs and LSIs

- **Use GSIs when**:
  - You need to query data using a partition key different from the base table's primary key.
  - Your queries require multiple access patterns and indexes on non-primary key attributes.
  - You need more flexibility and can afford eventual consistency for your queries.

- **Use LSIs when**:
  - You need to keep the same partition key and only modify the sort key.
  - You require strong consistency for queries.
  - You want to use multiple sort orders without changing the partition key.

7.2.4 Best Practices for Indexes

- **Minimize the Number of Indexes**: Each index consumes resources and incurs costs. Only create indexes for attributes that are frequently queried or are important for performance.
- **Monitor Index Usage**: Use CloudWatch and DynamoDB's metrics to monitor index performance. Remove unused or underperforming indexes to reduce costs and improve efficiency.
- **Design with Access Patterns in Mind**: When designing your table and indexes, carefully consider your application's access patterns. Plan your indexes around your most frequent queries to avoid costly and unnecessary scans.

Optimizing DynamoDB for high performance is essential for building scalable applications. Understanding **partitions**, **partition keys**, and **sort keys** allows you to design efficient data models that scale with your application's growth. Choosing the right **indexes**—whether **Global Secondary Indexes (GSI)** or **Local Secondary Indexes (LSI)**—ensures that your queries are fast and cost-effective, giving you the flexibility to access data in various ways without compromising performance. By applying these best practices, you can ensure that your DynamoDB-backed API performs optimally under high load, delivering a fast, responsive experience for your users.

7.3 Reducing Read and Write Costs

As you scale your application with DynamoDB, controlling costs while maintaining performance becomes increasingly important. DynamoDB offers several ways to optimize your read and write operations to reduce costs, without compromising on performance. Understanding the pricing model and how to optimize your API for cost efficiency is key to building a sustainable system.

7.3.1 DynamoDB Pricing Model

DynamoDB's pricing model is based on **read and write capacity units, data storage**, and **data transfer**. The main components are:

- **Provisioned Mode**: You specify the amount of read and write capacity (measured in read and write capacity units) that your application requires. You are billed based on the provisioned throughput, regardless of actual usage.
- **On-Demand Mode**: DynamoDB automatically adjusts the read and write throughput based on traffic patterns. You pay for actual requests rather than pre-provisioning capacity, which is beneficial for applications with unpredictable traffic.
- **Data Storage**: DynamoDB charges based on the amount of data you store in the database, including both indexed and non-indexed data.
- **Data Transfer**: You are billed for data transferred in and out of DynamoDB, with data transfers within the same AWS region being free, but cross-region or out-of-region data transfer incurring additional costs.

7.3.2 Strategies to Reduce Read and Write Costs

1. **Optimize Read and Write Capacity**:
   - If you are using **Provisioned Mode**, carefully monitor your application's read and write capacity requirements using **AWS CloudWatch** metrics. Adjust the provisioned throughput to avoid over-provisioning and unnecessary costs.
   - For **On-Demand Mode**, while there's no upfront capacity cost, avoid excessive reads and writes by optimizing your queries and write operations.
2. **Efficient Querying with Indexes**:
   - Avoid **full table scans** by using **Global Secondary Indexes (GSI)** or **Local Secondary Indexes (LSI)** to make queries more efficient and reduce the number of read operations. Indexes ensure that your queries don't need to scan the entire table, saving both time and cost.
   - Use **Query** operations instead of **Scan** operations whenever possible. A **Scan** operation reads the entire table, which is more expensive in terms of both cost and time, while a **Query** operation uses the index and is more cost-efficient.
3. **Leverage Batch Operations**:
   - Use **BatchWriteItem** and **BatchGetItem** operations to perform multiple writes or reads in a single API call. These batch operations reduce the

number of network calls, thus improving performance and potentially lowering costs.

Example of BatchGetItem:
python
Copy
```
response = dynamodb.batch_get_item(

    RequestItems={

        'Users': {

            'Keys': [

                {'userID': 'user123'},

                {'userID': 'user456'}

            ]

        }

    }

)
```

4. **Use DynamoDB Streams and AWS Lambda:**
   o To reduce write operations and automate business logic, consider using **DynamoDB Streams** in combination with **AWS Lambda**. DynamoDB Streams allows you to capture changes to your table and trigger Lambda functions that can process data asynchronously, reducing the need for frequent write operations.
5. **Leverage Conditional Writes:**
   o Use **conditional writes** (e.g., PutItem with a condition) to avoid unnecessary writes when the data has not changed. This ensures you don't overwrite existing data unless necessary, which can reduce costs for write-heavy applications.
6. **Efficient Use of Items:**
   o Make sure that you are only storing the necessary attributes in your items. Extra attributes increase storage costs and slow down read and

write operations. Minimize the data being stored and retrieved to only what is required for your application's functionality.

7. **Time-to-Live (TTL) for Expired Data**:
   o DynamoDB supports **Time to Live (TTL)**, a feature that automatically deletes expired items from your table. Setting up TTL ensures that obsolete data does not accumulate, reducing storage costs and improving read and write performance by keeping the table lean.

7.4 Best Practices for Scaling DynamoDB

DynamoDB is designed to scale automatically based on your application's needs. However, understanding how to scale it effectively will ensure that your application remains responsive and cost-effective as traffic increases. This section covers best practices for scaling your DynamoDB implementation to handle high-volume applications.

7.4.1 Horizontal Scaling with Partitions

DynamoDB automatically partitions data across multiple servers to manage large volumes of data. However, the way you design your partition keys directly impacts how efficiently your data is distributed across partitions.

- **Avoid Hot Partitions**: When a disproportionate number of requests are directed to a single partition key, it creates a "hot partition." This results in throttling and degraded performance. To avoid this, choose partition keys with high cardinality (a wide range of unique values). For example, using userID as the partition key is better than city in a global application.
- **Design for Scale**: Plan your access patterns and ensure that frequently queried data is well distributed across partitions. For example, if you have a table with orderID as the partition key, queries for orders from a specific customer (with many orders) could overload a partition. Instead, use a composite key with userID as the partition key and timestamp as the sort key to distribute the data.

7.4.2 Optimize Throughput with Auto Scaling

DynamoDB offers an **auto-scaling** feature that automatically adjusts the read and write capacity based on demand. Auto-scaling ensures that your application can handle varying traffic loads without manual intervention.

- **Enable Auto Scaling**: Set up auto-scaling for both read and write capacity in **Provisioned Mode**. This will allow DynamoDB to scale capacity automatically based on actual usage, helping to avoid throttling during peak loads.
- **Define Scaling Policies**: Configure the scaling policy to specify the upper and lower limits for your table's throughput. For example, you can set a range of capacity units and define the threshold for increasing or decreasing the capacity.

7.4.3 Use On-Demand Mode for Unpredictable Traffic

For workloads with unpredictable or variable traffic, consider using **On-Demand Mode**, which allows DynamoDB to automatically scale up and down without the need for provisioning capacity in advance.

- **On-Demand Mode Advantages**: On-demand mode is ideal for unpredictable workloads because it automatically adapts to changing traffic patterns. With no capacity planning required, it is easier to scale applications up or down based on actual request volume.
- **Cost Considerations**: While On-Demand Mode is convenient, it may not always be the most cost-effective choice for predictable workloads. Carefully analyze your traffic patterns to determine the best approach (Provisioned Mode vs. On-Demand Mode).

7.4.4 Partitioning Strategies for Large Datasets

For large datasets, ensure that your table design takes full advantage of DynamoDB's partitioning mechanism. DynamoDB automatically manages partitions behind the scenes, but there are design choices that can help optimize partitioning:

- **Distribute Traffic Evenly**: Avoid using highly skewed partition keys, as they can create uneven data distribution. When partition keys are poorly distributed, it results in **hot partitions** that can overload a single partition and degrade performance.
- **Composite Keys for Range Queries**: Use composite keys (partition key + sort key) to enable efficient range queries. This helps DynamoDB distribute data more evenly across partitions, improving query performance.

7.4.5 Global Tables for Multi-Region Applications

If your application needs to be globally available, consider using **Global Tables**. Global Tables allow you to replicate your DynamoDB table across multiple AWS regions for low-latency, high-availability access.

- **Use Cases for Global Tables**: Global Tables are ideal for applications that need to serve users in multiple geographic regions with low-latency read and write operations. Examples include social networks, e-commerce platforms, and financial applications.

7.5 Monitoring and Troubleshooting DynamoDB APIs

Effective monitoring and troubleshooting are essential for maintaining the health and performance of your DynamoDB-based application. AWS provides several tools and best practices to help monitor DynamoDB performance and diagnose issues as they arise.

7.5.1 CloudWatch Metrics for DynamoDB

Amazon **CloudWatch** provides metrics that help monitor the health and performance of DynamoDB tables and indexes. These metrics help you identify bottlenecks, throttling events, and other potential issues.

Key CloudWatch Metrics to Monitor:

- **ConsumedReadCapacityUnits**: Measures the number of read capacity units consumed by your table or index. High values may indicate that your read capacity is being over-utilized.
- **ConsumedWriteCapacityUnits**: Measures the number of write capacity units consumed. High values may indicate that your write throughput is being throttled.
- **ThrottledRequests**: Indicates the number of requests that have been throttled due to insufficient throughput. If this value is consistently high, you may need to adjust your provisioned throughput or switch to On-Demand Mode.
- **ProvisionedThroughputExceeded**: A measure of the number of times DynamoDB exceeds the provisioned throughput limits. This is critical for diagnosing bottlenecks or hot partitions.

- **ReturnedItemCount**: The number of items returned by a query or scan. This can help identify whether your queries are returning too much data, which may indicate inefficient queries.

7.5.2 DynamoDB Streams for Troubleshooting

DynamoDB Streams capture changes to items in your DynamoDB tables and can be used for real-time processing or debugging.

- **Use Streams to Track Changes**: Enable DynamoDB Streams to capture data modifications (inserts, updates, deletes) in your table. You can then process these events using **AWS Lambda** to analyze and track changes, audit user actions, or troubleshoot specific issues.

Example: Integrating DynamoDB Streams with Lambda:
python
Copy
```
import boto3


dynamodb = boto3.client('dynamodb')


def process_stream(event, context):

    for record in event['Records']:

        print(record)  # Process the record from the stream
```

7.5.3 Troubleshooting Performance Issues

1. **Throttling Issues**:
   - If your application is experiencing **throttling**, check for high values in **ConsumedReadCapacityUnits** or **ConsumedWriteCapacityUnits** metrics in CloudWatch. This indicates that the read or write capacity may need to be increased or optimized.

2. **Hot Partitions**:
   - If you notice that one partition is receiving an inordinate amount of traffic (indicated by high **ConsumedReadCapacityUnits** on a specific partition), consider redesigning your partition key to distribute traffic more evenly.
3. **Slow Queries**:
   - Review the queries that are causing high **Read/Write Capacity Consumption** or high **ReturnedItemCount** values. Consider optimizing your data model by creating secondary indexes or using more efficient query operations like Query instead of Scan.

4. **Using the AWS DynamoDB Console**:
   - The **DynamoDB Console** provides built-in troubleshooting tools such as **table health monitoring, query performance analysis**, and the ability to view table and index consumption metrics.

Chapter 8: Optimizing PostgreSQL for High Performance

8.1 Query Optimization Techniques

Query optimization is one of the most crucial aspects of ensuring high performance in a PostgreSQL-based system. Without effective query optimization, even a well-structured database can suffer from slow performance, especially when handling large datasets or complex queries. PostgreSQL provides a range of tools and techniques to optimize the execution of SQL queries, improve response times, and reduce server load. In this section, we will explore several query optimization strategies that can help you achieve high performance for your PostgreSQL database.

8.1.1 Analyzing Query Performance

Before you can optimize queries, you need to understand where the performance bottlenecks lie. PostgreSQL provides several ways to analyze the performance of your queries, which is the first step in the optimization process.

EXPLAIN Command: The **EXPLAIN** command in PostgreSQL shows the execution plan of a query, which provides insights into how the database engine processes the query. The output includes details such as the order in which tables are scanned, whether indexes are being used, and the estimated cost of each operation. Using EXPLAIN ANALYZE will not only give you the plan but also the actual time taken by each step. Example:
sql
Copy
EXPLAIN ANALYZE SELECT * FROM orders WHERE customer_id = 123;

This command will output the query execution plan, helping you identify areas for improvement. Look for any **Sequential Scans** or **Full Table Scans**, as these are often indications that indexing or query structure needs improvement.

pg_stat_statements: PostgreSQL's **pg_stat_statements** extension tracks execution statistics for all SQL statements executed by the database. By enabling this extension, you can gather valuable metrics about query frequency, execution time, and resource consumption, which can be used to identify slow or frequently executed queries that may need optimization.

To enable **pg_stat_statements**:

sql

Copy

```
CREATE EXTENSION pg_stat_statements;
```

After enabling the extension, you can view query statistics with:

sql

Copy

```
SELECT * FROM pg_stat_statements ORDER BY total_time DESC LIMIT 10;
```

> This query will return the top 10 queries that have taken the most time, which helps in identifying performance bottlenecks.

8.1.2 Reducing Complexity of Queries

Complex queries with multiple **JOINs**, subqueries, and aggregates can often lead to poor performance if not optimized. Here are some techniques to reduce the complexity and improve the efficiency of your queries:

Avoid SELECT *: Using SELECT * returns all columns from a table, which can be inefficient, especially if you only need a subset of the columns. Always specify only the necessary columns in your queries.

Example:

sql

Copy

```
SELECT id, order_date, total_amount FROM orders WHERE customer_id = 123;
```

> This query retrieves only the columns that are required, which reduces the amount of data being processed and transferred.

Limit the Result Set: When dealing with large tables, always limit the number of rows returned when possible. You can use the LIMIT clause to restrict the result set to only the necessary rows, which can significantly improve performance.

Example:

sql

Copy

```
SELECT * FROM orders WHERE customer_id = 123 ORDER BY order_date DESC LIMIT 10;
```

> This query fetches only the 10 most recent orders for a customer.

Use Proper Filtering and Indexing: Make sure that your queries are well-filtered, and ensure that appropriate indexes are in place. Inefficient filters (such as applying complex expressions or functions to the columns in the WHERE clause) can prevent PostgreSQL from using indexes effectively.

Example:

sql

Copy

```
SELECT * FROM orders WHERE order_date >= '2022-01-01' AND customer_id = 123;
```

1. In this query, the filters on order_date and customer_id can be optimized by indexing both columns, making the query faster.
2. **Optimize Subqueries and Joins**: Subqueries and joins are often a source of inefficiency. Always aim to simplify them where possible:
    - **Use JOIN efficiently**: Ensure that the join conditions are indexed and avoid unnecessary joins.
    - **Consider WITH clauses**: In some cases, you may benefit from using **Common Table Expressions (CTEs)** or **WITH** clauses, which can break down complex queries into more manageable steps.

Example using a CTE:

sql

Copy

```
WITH customer_orders AS (
    SELECT customer_id, COUNT(*) AS order_count
    FROM orders
    GROUP BY customer_id
)
SELECT customer_id, order_count FROM customer_orders WHERE order_count > 5;
```

3. This breaks down a complex query into a simpler form and can improve performance by reusing the intermediate result set.
4. **Use Index-Only Scans**: An **Index-Only Scan** is a query execution plan where PostgreSQL can retrieve all necessary data from the index alone, without having to access the underlying table. This significantly speeds up query execution.
   To take advantage of this, ensure that your queries only request columns that are part of the index. For instance, if you're querying a table by a date range and only need the date and ID columns, make sure the index includes those columns.

8.2 Indexing Strategies for Fast Lookups

Indexing is one of the most powerful tools for improving query performance in PostgreSQL. An index allows the database to locate data quickly without scanning the entire table. However, improper or excessive indexing can negatively affect performance, so it's crucial to choose the right indexes and apply them effectively.

8.2.1 Types of Indexes in PostgreSQL

PostgreSQL supports several types of indexes, each with specific use cases. Understanding the different types of indexes and how to use them can dramatically improve the performance of your queries.

B-tree Indexes (Default Index Type): The default index type in PostgreSQL is the **B-tree** index. B-tree indexes are best for equality comparisons ($=$) and range queries ($<$, $<=$, $>$, $>=$). These are ideal for indexing columns that are frequently used in WHERE clauses or as join conditions.
Example:
sql
Copy

```
CREATE INDEX idx_customer_id ON orders(customer_id);
```

This index would improve queries filtering by customer_id:
sql
Copy

```
SELECT * FROM orders WHERE customer_id = 123;
```

1. **Hash Indexes**: **Hash indexes** are specialized for equality comparisons but are less commonly used than B-tree indexes because they do not support range queries. Hash indexes are suitable for applications that require exact-match lookups with equality operators.
   Example:
   sql
   Copy

   ```
   CREATE INDEX idx_hash_customer_id ON orders USING hash (customer_id);
   ```

   Use this type of index only for queries that use exact match ($=$) comparisons.

GIN (Generalized Inverted Index) and GiST (Generalized Search Tree) Indexes: **GIN** and **GiST** indexes are used for more specialized use cases such as full-text search,

101

arrays, and geometric data types. GIN is ideal for indexing array columns or text search, whereas GiST is useful for indexing geometric data types.

Example (for full-text search):

sql

Copy

```sql
CREATE INDEX idx_fulltext_search ON articles USING gin(to_tsvector('english', content));
```

BRIN (Block Range INdexes): **BRIN indexes** are designed for large tables where the data is naturally ordered, such as time-series data or large logs. BRIN indexes are much smaller than traditional B-tree indexes and are faster to create and update, but they are less precise and are better suited to queries that scan large ranges of data.

Example:

sql

Copy

```sql
CREATE INDEX idx_brin ON large_table USING brin (timestamp);
```

> This index would be beneficial for time-series data where queries typically look for ranges of timestamps.

8.2.2 When to Use Indexes

Frequently Queried Columns: Index columns that are frequently used in query filters, joins, and sorting operations. If a column is used repeatedly in WHERE clauses or ORDER BY statements, creating an index can significantly speed up queries.

Example:

sql

Copy

```sql
CREATE INDEX idx_product_name ON products(name);
```

Composite Indexes: If your queries filter or sort on multiple columns, consider creating **composite indexes** (indexes on more than one column). Composite indexes allow PostgreSQL to efficiently handle queries that use multiple filter conditions.

Example:

sql

Copy

```sql
CREATE INDEX idx_order_customer_date ON orders(customer_id, order_date);
```

102

This index would optimize queries filtering by both customer_id and order_date.

Covering Indexes: A **covering index** is one where the index itself contains all the columns needed for the query, meaning PostgreSQL can satisfy the query using just the index without having to access the underlying table. For this to happen, the indexed columns must include all the columns used in the SELECT, WHERE, ORDER BY, or GROUP BY clauses.
Example:
sql
Copy
```
CREATE INDEX idx_order_customer_date_status ON orders(customer_id, order_date, status);
```

This composite index would allow a query filtering by customer_id, order_date, and status to be answered entirely using the index.

8.2.3 Index Maintenance

Creating indexes is just the beginning; you must also maintain them to ensure they continue to perform well:

Avoid Over-Indexing: While indexes improve read performance, they add overhead to insert and update operations because the index must be updated whenever the data in the table changes. Avoid creating unnecessary indexes, and periodically review them to ensure they are still needed.

Rebuild Indexes: Over time, as data changes, indexes can become fragmented. Running the REINDEX command periodically can help optimize the performance of your indexes.
Example:
sql
Copy
```
REINDEX INDEX idx_customer_id;
```

Monitor Index Usage: Use PostgreSQL's system views like pg_stat_user_indexes to monitor how often indexes are used. If an index is rarely used, it might be best to drop it to save on storage and update costs.
Example:
sql
Copy
SELECT * FROM pg_stat_user_indexes WHERE idx_scan = 0;

Consider Partial Indexes: A **partial index** is an index that only includes rows that meet a certain condition, which can reduce the index size and improve performance when only a subset of the data is frequently queried.
Example:
sql
Copy
CREATE INDEX idx_active_orders ON orders (customer_id) WHERE status = 'active';

> This index will only index rows where status = 'active', making it more efficient for queries that focus on active orders.

Optimizing PostgreSQL for high performance requires a combination of effective query optimization techniques and thoughtful indexing strategies. By analyzing query performance with tools like **EXPLAIN** and **pg_stat_statements**, reducing the complexity of queries, and applying the right types of indexes (such as B-tree, GIN, and BRIN), you can significantly improve both query speed and overall database performance. Furthermore, maintaining a lean set of indexes, monitoring their usage, and periodically optimizing them will ensure that your PostgreSQL database can handle high volumes of data while providing fast, responsive query execution.

8.3 Connection Pooling for Performance

In a high-traffic application, efficiently managing database connections is critical to ensuring that your PostgreSQL database can handle large numbers of concurrent queries without overwhelming the system. **Connection pooling** is a technique that helps manage the number of active database connections, reducing the overhead of establishing a new connection for each query.

8.3.1 What is Connection Pooling?

Connection pooling involves maintaining a pool of reusable database connections that can be shared among multiple application requests. Instead of opening and closing a new connection to the database each time a query is made, the application can request an available connection from the pool. This significantly reduces the time spent on connection establishment and teardown, which is especially important for high-performance systems that handle many concurrent connections.

8.3.2 Why Use Connection Pooling?

- **Improved Performance**: Creating a new database connection for each query can be time-consuming, particularly when the database is hosted remotely. Connection pooling minimizes this overhead by reusing existing connections.
- **Resource Management**: Connection pooling ensures that the number of active connections to the database remains within a manageable range. This prevents the database from becoming overwhelmed by too many simultaneous connections, which could lead to performance degradation or even crashes.
- **Reduced Latency**: By reusing connections, the time spent establishing and tearing down database connections is eliminated, which reduces query latency.
- **Efficient Database Resource Utilization**: Pooling allows for better control of the number of open connections, ensuring that the database's resources are used efficiently without exceeding its maximum allowed connection limit.

8.3.3 Setting Up Connection Pooling in PostgreSQL

PostgreSQL itself doesn't include a built-in connection pooler, but you can use external tools like **pgBouncer** or **PgPool** to manage connection pooling effectively.

Using pgBouncer

pgBouncer is a lightweight connection pooler for PostgreSQL that handles client connections, reduces the overhead of establishing new connections, and can help with load balancing.

Install pgBouncer:
bash
Copy
sudo apt-get install pgbouncer

1. **Configure pgBouncer**: Once installed, configure the pgbouncer.ini file to specify the database connections and pool size. Key parameters to configure include:
   - **pool_size**: Defines the maximum number of connections that can be pooled.
   - **max_client_conn**: Specifies the maximum number of client connections pgBouncer will accept.

Example:
ini
Copy
[databases]
mydatabase = host=localhost dbname=mydatabase user=myuser password=mypassword

[pgbouncer]
pool_size = 20
max_client_conn = 100

2. **Start pgBouncer**: Start the pgBouncer service to begin pooling connections.
   bash
   Copy
   sudo systemctl start pgbouncer

3. **Use the Pool**: Once pgBouncer is set up, applications connect to it instead of connecting directly to PostgreSQL. pgBouncer will handle managing and reusing connections as needed.

Using PgPool

PgPool is another popular connection pooling tool that provides more advanced features such as load balancing, query caching, and failover support.

Install PgPool:
bash
Copy
sudo apt-get install pgpool2

1. **Configure PgPool**: After installation, configure the pgpool.conf file to adjust the connection pool settings.
   Key parameters:
   - **num_init_children**: The number of child processes that pgPool will spawn to handle connections.
   - **max_pool**: Defines the number of backend connections that each child process can handle.
   - **listen_addresses**: Specifies the network interfaces where pgPool should listen for incoming connections.

Example:
ini
Copy
num_init_children = 32
max_pool = 4
listen_addresses = '*'

2. **Start PgPool**:
bash
Copy
sudo systemctl start pgpool2

2. **Use the Pool**: Similar to pgBouncer, applications will now connect to PgPool instead of connecting directly to PostgreSQL, allowing PgPool to manage connection pooling and load balancing.

8.3.4 Best Practices for Connection Pooling

- **Adjust Pool Size Based on Traffic**: The pool size should be configured based on your application's expected traffic. Having too few connections in the pool can lead to connection timeouts, while too many can overwhelm the database server.

107

- **Use Persistent Connections**: Reusing connections for as long as possible within a transaction or session improves efficiency and reduces overhead.
- **Use Connection Pooling with Read-Write Splitting**: In applications where read-heavy operations are prevalent, consider using a connection pooler with support for **read-write splitting**, where read queries are directed to read replicas and write queries go to the primary database.

8.4 Advanced Configuration and Tuning

PostgreSQL provides a range of configuration options that can help fine-tune the database's performance for different workloads. In this section, we'll cover some of the most important configurations for optimizing PostgreSQL performance.

8.4.1 Shared Buffers

Shared Buffers define the amount of memory PostgreSQL uses to cache data in memory before reading or writing it to disk. The larger the shared buffer pool, the more data PostgreSQL can hold in memory, reducing the number of disk reads.

Configuration: The shared buffer size is set in the postgresql.conf file with the shared_buffers parameter.
Example:
ini
Copy
shared_buffers = 4GB

- **Best Practice**: Set shared_buffers to about **25-40%** of your total available memory, depending on the workload. Increasing shared buffers can significantly improve performance, especially for read-heavy workloads.

8.4.2 Work Mem

Work Mem is the amount of memory PostgreSQL allocates for operations such as sorting and joining tables. Increasing the work_mem setting can speed up these operations, but too high a value can lead to memory issues.

Configuration: Set work_mem to a value that allows efficient processing of queries without consuming excessive memory.

Example:
ini
Copy
work_mem = 64MB

-
- **Best Practice**: Set work_mem high enough to avoid on-disk sorting but low enough to ensure that the server does not run out of memory when handling multiple concurrent queries.

8.4.3 Maintenance Work Mem

Maintenance Work Mem is similar to work_mem, but it specifically affects maintenance operations such as **VACUUM, CREATE INDEX**, and **ALTER TABLE**.

Configuration:
ini
Copy
maintenance_work_mem = 512MB

- **Best Practice**: Increase this setting when performing large database maintenance operations, such as reindexing or vacuuming large tables.

8.4.4 Autovacuum

PostgreSQL uses **autovacuum** to automatically clean up dead tuples (stale rows) left behind by **UPDATE** or **DELETE** operations. Proper configuration of autovacuum is essential for maintaining database performance, especially in systems with high write activity.

Configuration: Enable and fine-tune autovacuum parameters in postgresql.conf.
Example:
ini
Copy
autovacuum = on
autovacuum_naptime = 10min

- **Best Practice**: Enable autovacuum and adjust the frequency of vacuuming based on table size and write activity. Increase the autovacuum_vacuum_scale_factor for large tables to reduce the frequency of vacuuming, but ensure that tables do not accumulate excessive dead tuples.

8.4.5 Effective Cache Size

Effective Cache Size informs the query planner about the amount of memory available for caching data. Setting this value correctly helps PostgreSQL make better decisions about which execution plans to choose.

Configuration: Set the effective_cache_size parameter to reflect the memory available for caching (including OS-level caches).
Example:
ini
Copy
effective_cache_size = 12GB

- **Best Practice**: Set this parameter to roughly **50-75%** of the total system memory, depending on the workload and the system's usage of other resources.

8.5 Monitoring and Troubleshooting PostgreSQL APIs

Once you've optimized PostgreSQL for high performance, ongoing monitoring is essential to ensure the system continues to function efficiently. Monitoring tools can help detect issues such as slow queries, high resource consumption, and performance bottlenecks.

8.5.1 Key Metrics to Monitor

1. **Query Performance**: Use the EXPLAIN ANALYZE command and tools like **pg_stat_statements** to identify slow queries and understand how the database is processing them.
   - **Slow Queries**: Track queries that take longer to execute than expected and optimize them using indexes or better query structure.
   - **Query Execution Time**: Monitor query execution times to ensure that your queries are performing efficiently.
2. **Database I/O**: Monitor the **I/O performance** of PostgreSQL, particularly disk usage and disk reads/writes. High disk usage can indicate that your shared_buffers or work_mem settings need adjustment.

3. **Memory Usage**: Track memory usage by monitoring **shared_buffers**, **work_mem**, and **maintenance_work_mem** to ensure that PostgreSQL isn't using excessive memory, which could impact performance or lead to system crashes.

Locks and Deadlocks: Monitor for **locks** and **deadlocks** to ensure that queries are not being blocked by other transactions. PostgreSQL provides system views such as pg_locks and pg_stat_activity to monitor locking issues.
Example:
sql
Copy
SELECT * FROM pg_stat_activity WHERE state = 'active';

Autovacuum Activity: Check autovacuum activity to ensure that dead tuples are being cleared regularly. If autovacuum is not running frequently enough, database performance may degrade over time.
Example:
sql
Copy
SELECT * FROM pg_stat_user_tables WHERE last_vacuum IS NULL;

8.5.2 Troubleshooting Common Issues

1. **Slow Queries**: Slow queries are often the result of missing indexes or inefficient query structures. Use the **EXPLAIN ANALYZE** command to identify whether the query is using indexes and adjust the query or indexes accordingly.
2. **High Latency**: High query latency can occur when the database has to perform **full table scans** or when there are not enough resources (memory, CPU) to handle the query load. Improve indexing, increase cache sizes, and optimize queries to reduce latency.
3. **Database Overload**: If your database is overloaded and queries are being throttled, consider scaling your infrastructure (e.g., adding read replicas for load balancing) or optimizing queries and indexes.
4. **Connection Problems**: High connection counts or connection pooling issues can lead to database overload. Use tools like **pgBouncer** for connection pooling, and monitor connection usage via **pg_stat_activity**.

8.5.3 Using Third-Party Monitoring Tools

In addition to PostgreSQL's native tools, several third-party monitoring solutions provide advanced features for tracking database health and performance. These tools can give you a deeper insight into the database's performance and provide detailed metrics, real-time alerts, and historical data analysis.

Popular monitoring tools include:

- **pgAdmin**: A popular web-based GUI for PostgreSQL administration that also includes basic performance monitoring.
- **Datadog**: A powerful monitoring service that integrates with PostgreSQL and provides detailed insights into performance, queries, and database health.
- **Prometheus and Grafana**: Open-source tools for collecting and visualizing PostgreSQL metrics, allowing for real-time monitoring and custom alerts.

Chapter 9: Integrating with Cloud Platforms

9.1 Integrating DynamoDB with AWS Lambda and API Gateway

Amazon Web Services (AWS) offers a variety of tools that can be seamlessly integrated with **DynamoDB** to build scalable and efficient cloud-based applications. Among the most popular integrations are **AWS Lambda** and **API Gateway**, which together allow you to build serverless applications that are highly performant, cost-efficient, and easy to scale. In this section, we'll explore how to integrate **DynamoDB** with **AWS Lambda** and **API Gateway** for a seamless serverless architecture.

9.1.1 What is AWS Lambda?

AWS Lambda is a compute service that allows you to run code without provisioning or managing servers. You upload your code, specify the event that should trigger it (such as an API request or a DynamoDB stream), and Lambda automatically executes the code in response to the event. Lambda is particularly useful in serverless architectures because it eliminates the need to manage infrastructure, scaling automatically based on the amount of requests.

9.1.2 What is API Gateway?

Amazon API Gateway is a fully managed service that enables you to create, deploy, and manage APIs for your applications. API Gateway acts as the entry point for client applications to interact with the backend services. It supports both RESTful APIs and WebSocket APIs, providing tools for throttling, authorization, and monitoring. By integrating API Gateway with Lambda, you can quickly expose your DynamoDB-backed data to clients through a secure and scalable API.

9.1.3 Benefits of Integrating DynamoDB with AWS Lambda and API Gateway

- **Serverless Architecture**: With Lambda and API Gateway, you can build a fully serverless application that scales automatically based on incoming requests without needing to manage any servers.
- **Event-Driven**: DynamoDB streams can trigger Lambda functions whenever there are changes to the data, allowing you to react to changes in real-time.
- **Cost-Efficiency**: AWS Lambda charges based on the number of invocations and the duration of code execution, while API Gateway charges based on the number of API calls. This means you only pay for the resources you actually use, making it highly cost-effective for variable or low-traffic applications.

9.1.4 Setting Up DynamoDB, Lambda, and API Gateway Integration

Let's walk through how you can integrate DynamoDB with Lambda and API Gateway to expose DynamoDB data via an API.

Step 1: Create a DynamoDB Table

1. Log in to the AWS Console and navigate to the DynamoDB service.
2. Click **Create table**.
3. Specify a table name (e.g., Users) and a primary key (e.g., userID as the partition key).
4. Set the desired read and write capacity or enable **on-demand mode**.

Step 2: Create an AWS Lambda Function

1. Navigate to **AWS Lambda** in the console and click **Create function**.
2. Choose **Author from Scratch** and provide a function name (e.g., GetUserFunction).
3. Set the runtime to **Node.js**, **Python**, or another preferred language.

In the function's code editor, write code to interact with the DynamoDB table. For example, here's a simple Node.js function to retrieve a user by userID:
javascript
Copy

```javascript
const AWS = require('aws-sdk');
const dynamoDb = new AWS.DynamoDB.DocumentClient();

exports.handler = async (event) => {
  const userId = event.pathParameters.userID;
  const params = {
    TableName: 'Users',
    Key: {
      userID: userId,
    },
  };

  try {
    const result = await dynamoDb.get(params).promise();
    if (result.Item) {
      return {
```

```
        statusCode: 200,
        body: JSON.stringify(result.Item),
      };
    } else {
      return {
        statusCode: 404,
        body: JSON.stringify({ message: 'User not found' }),
      };
    }
  } catch (error) {
    return {
      statusCode: 500,
      body: JSON.stringify({ message: 'Internal Server Error' }),
    };
  }
};
```

Step 3: Configure Lambda Permissions

1. Your Lambda function needs permission to read from the DynamoDB table. Attach an **IAM role** to the Lambda function with the dynamodb:GetItem permission.
2. Go to the **IAM Role** section, create a new role, and attach the necessary policy to allow Lambda to interact with DynamoDB.

Step 4: Create an API in API Gateway

1. Navigate to **Amazon API Gateway** in the console and click **Create API**.
2. Choose **REST API** and select **New API**.
3. Create a resource (e.g., /users), and under that, create a new method (e.g., GET).
4. Set the integration type to **Lambda Function** and select the Lambda function (GetUserFunction) you created earlier.
5. Deploy the API to a new stage, such as **dev**.

Step 5: Test the Integration

1. After deploying the API, you will receive a **URL** that you can use to make requests.

Test the API by making a GET request to:
php-template
Copy
https://<api-id>.execute-api.<region>.amazonaws.com/dev/users/{userID}

2. Replace {userID} with an actual userID value that exists in your DynamoDB table.
3. You should see the retrieved user data in the response.

Step 6: Monitor and Secure the API

- **Monitoring**: Use **Amazon CloudWatch** to monitor Lambda executions and API Gateway performance. You can track metrics such as execution time, errors, and invocations.
- **Security**: Secure your API with **AWS IAM**, **API keys**, or **Cognito** for user authentication.

9.2 Using AWS RDS for PostgreSQL Deployment

For applications requiring a relational database management system (RDBMS) like **PostgreSQL**, AWS provides the **Amazon RDS (Relational Database Service)**. RDS simplifies the setup, operation, and scaling of a PostgreSQL database, allowing you to focus on application development rather than database management. In this section, we'll explore how to deploy and optimize PostgreSQL using AWS RDS.

9.2.1 What is AWS RDS?

Amazon RDS is a fully managed relational database service that supports multiple database engines, including PostgreSQL. With RDS, AWS handles administrative tasks such as backups, patching, scaling, and monitoring, enabling you to focus on your application rather than database management. RDS also provides features like automatic backups, multi-Availability Zone (AZ) replication, and read replicas for improved performance and high availability.

9.2.2 Benefits of Using RDS for PostgreSQL

1. **Fully Managed**: AWS takes care of database maintenance tasks, such as software patching and backups, reducing administrative overhead.
2. **Scalability**: You can scale your database up or down with just a few clicks, either by resizing the instance or adding read replicas for improved read throughput.
3. **High Availability**: Amazon RDS supports **Multi-AZ deployments**, providing automatic failover in case of primary instance failure. This ensures your database remains available with minimal downtime.
4. **Security**: RDS integrates with **IAM** for access control and **VPC** for network isolation, providing secure communication between your application and the database.
5. **Automatic Backups**: RDS automatically backs up your PostgreSQL databases and enables point-in-time recovery.

9.2.3 Deploying PostgreSQL with AWS RDS

Let's walk through how to deploy a PostgreSQL database on AWS RDS.

Step 1: Create an RDS Instance for PostgreSQL

1. Log in to the **AWS Management Console** and navigate to **RDS**.
2. Click on **Create database** and select **Standard Create**.
3. Choose **PostgreSQL** as the database engine.
4. Configure the database instance settings:
   - **DB Instance Identifier**: Choose a name for your database instance (e.g., my-postgres-db).
   - **Master Username**: Set the username for the database (e.g., admin).
   - **Master Password**: Set a secure password for the database.
5. Choose the desired instance type and size based on your application's requirements. You can choose from different instance classes, such as db.t3.micro for small workloads or db.m5.large for larger applications.
6. Set the **Storage** and **Backup** options based on your needs, including enabling **Automated backups** and **Multi-AZ deployments** for high availability.

Step 2: Configure Network and Security

1. **VPC**: Choose the Virtual Private Cloud (VPC) where your RDS instance will reside. This ensures that your database is isolated from the public internet.

2. **Security Group**: Configure a security group that allows access to the database instance from specific IP addresses or other resources within your VPC. For example, you can allow connections from your application server or EC2 instances.

Step 3: Launch the RDS Instance

1. Review all settings, and click **Create database** to launch the PostgreSQL instance.
2. Once the instance is created, it will be assigned an **endpoint** that you can use to connect to the database.

Step 4: Connect to the PostgreSQL Database

1. Use the **endpoint**, **master username**, and **password** to connect to your PostgreSQL database.
2. You can connect using any PostgreSQL client (e.g., **pgAdmin**, **psql**, or a programming language library like **psycopg2** for Python).

Example of connecting using psql:

bash
Copy
```
psql -h <endpoint> -U admin -d postgres
```

Step 5: Database Operations

Once connected, you can start performing regular database operations, such as creating tables, inserting data, and running queries.

Example:

sql
Copy
```
CREATE TABLE users (
    user_id SERIAL PRIMARY KEY,
    first_name VARCHAR(50),
    last_name VARCHAR(50),
    email VARCHAR(100) UNIQUE
);
```

Step 6: Monitoring and Backups

- **Monitoring**: Use **Amazon CloudWatch** to monitor RDS instance performance metrics such as CPU utilization, read/write latency, and disk I/O. You can set up alarms to notify you of any issues.
- **Backups**: AWS RDS automatically backs up your PostgreSQL database and retains backups for a specified retention period. You can also initiate manual backups or restore to a previous point-in-time.

9.2.4 Scaling PostgreSQL on AWS RDS

As your application grows, you may need to scale your PostgreSQL instance for higher performance and availability.

1. **Vertical Scaling**: You can resize the instance to a larger type with more CPU, memory, and storage. This can be done through the RDS console without downtime (for non-production environments).
2. **Horizontal Scaling**: Use **Read Replicas** to offload read-heavy queries from the primary database. AWS RDS supports the creation of read replicas in different regions to distribute the load and provide high availability.
3. **Automatic Scaling**: You can also configure **Auto Scaling** for the storage capacity of your RDS instance, ensuring that your database scales with the growing data needs.

9.3 Scaling with Cloud Services: Load Balancing, Autoscaling, and More

In cloud environments, scalability is key to ensuring that your applications can handle increasing loads while maintaining performance and availability. AWS provides several services to achieve **scalability**, including **load balancing**, **autoscaling**, and **elasticity**. In this section, we'll explore how to scale your application using these cloud services, ensuring it can dynamically adjust to varying traffic demands.

9.3.1 Load Balancing with Elastic Load Balancer (ELB)

Elastic Load Balancing (ELB) automatically distributes incoming application traffic across multiple targets, such as Amazon EC2 instances, Lambda functions, or containers, ensuring that no single resource is overwhelmed. ELB offers three types of load balancers:

1. **Application Load Balancer (ALB)**: Ideal for HTTP/HTTPS traffic, ALB operates at the application layer (Layer 7) and allows routing based on URL path, host headers, and more. It's well-suited for modern microservices architectures and containerized applications.
   Example: You can route traffic to different backend services based on the URL path:
   - /users routes to the user service.
   - /orders routes to the order service.
2. **Network Load Balancer (NLB)**: Operates at the transport layer (Layer 4) and is designed for high-performance, low-latency traffic. It's ideal for handling millions of requests per second while maintaining high throughput and static IP support.
3. **Classic Load Balancer (CLB)**: This is the legacy version of the load balancer, operating at both Layer 4 and Layer 7, used primarily for older applications.

9.3.2 Autoscaling with Amazon EC2 and Lambda

Autoscaling ensures that your application can automatically scale up or down based on traffic patterns. AWS provides several autoscaling options for both EC2 instances and Lambda functions:

1. **EC2 Auto Scaling**: With EC2 Auto Scaling, you can automatically adjust the number of EC2 instances in your application based on demand. Auto Scaling groups help maintain performance by launching new instances during high traffic and terminating instances when demand decreases.
   - **Scaling Policies**: You can configure scaling policies based on metrics such as CPU utilization, memory usage, or custom metrics from CloudWatch. For instance, if CPU utilization exceeds 80% for five minutes, auto-scaling can trigger the creation of a new EC2 instance.
   - **Launch Configurations**: When creating an Auto Scaling group, you define the **launch configuration** to specify the EC2 instance type, AMI, security groups, and key pairs.

Example:
bash
Copy

```
aws autoscaling create-auto-scaling-group --auto-scaling-group-name my-asg
```

--launch-configuration-name my-config --min-size 1 --max-size 10 --desired-capacity 5 --vpc-zone-identifier subnet-abc123

2. **Lambda Auto Scaling**: AWS Lambda automatically scales the execution of functions in response to incoming requests. As an event-driven serverless compute service, Lambda allows you to scale functions automatically and seamlessly without needing to configure scaling policies.
Lambda functions scale horizontally, meaning that multiple instances of the same function can run simultaneously if needed. There is no need to worry about resource allocation, as AWS Lambda handles the scaling based on the rate of incoming events (e.g., HTTP requests from API Gateway, changes in DynamoDB streams).

9.3.3 Elasticity with Amazon CloudWatch

Elasticity refers to the ability of a system to dynamically allocate resources based on real-time demand. **Amazon CloudWatch** is a monitoring service that provides real-time visibility into resource usage, application performance, and operational health.

Monitoring Resources: Use CloudWatch to monitor EC2 instance metrics like CPU utilization, disk I/O, and network traffic. Similarly, you can track Lambda metrics such as function invocation counts, duration, and error rates.

CloudWatch Alarms: You can create alarms to trigger actions based on resource thresholds, such as scaling up EC2 instances or sending notifications when specific metrics exceed a certain limit.
Example:
bash
Copy

```
aws cloudwatch put-metric-alarm --alarm-name HighCPUUtilization --metric-name CPUUtilization --namespace AWS/EC2 --statistic Average --period 300 --threshold 80 --comparison-operator GreaterThanThreshold --dimension Name=InstanceId,Value=i-1234567890 --evaluation-periods 2 --alarm-actions arn:aws:sns:us-west-2:123456789012:MyTopic
```

Elastic Load Balancing Integration: You can also integrate CloudWatch metrics with ELB to monitor the health of load balancers and automatically adjust traffic distribution.

9.4 Deploying Serverless APIs on AWS with DynamoDB

AWS allows developers to build **serverless APIs** that scale effortlessly, with minimal operational overhead. By combining **DynamoDB**, **AWS Lambda**, and **API Gateway**, you can quickly build powerful APIs that don't require server management. Let's walk through the process of deploying serverless APIs using DynamoDB.

9.4.1 What is a Serverless API?

A **serverless API** is an API that uses serverless computing services, such as AWS Lambda, for execution, eliminating the need for managing servers or infrastructure. The key benefits of serverless APIs include automatic scaling, reduced cost (pay-per-use), and easy integration with other AWS services.

9.4.2 Building the API with AWS Lambda and API Gateway

Create DynamoDB Table: First, create a **DynamoDB table** to store data. Let's assume the table is called Users with a userID partition key. This table will be used to store user information.

Create AWS Lambda Function: Write the Lambda function that will interact with DynamoDB. Lambda will handle the logic for reading and writing data from/to DynamoDB.
Example Lambda function in Python:
python
Copy

```
import json
import boto3
from botocore.exceptions import ClientError

dynamodb = boto3.resource('dynamodb')
table = dynamodb.Table('Users')

def lambda_handler(event, context):
    user_id = event['pathParameters']['userID']
    try:
        response = table.get_item(Key={'userID': user_id})
        if 'Item' in response:
            return {
                'statusCode': 200,
```

```
      'body': json.dumps(response['Item'])
    }
  else:
    return {
      'statusCode': 404,
      'body': json.dumps({'message': 'User not found'})
    }
except ClientError as e:
  return {
    'statusCode': 500,
    'body': json.dumps({'message': str(e)})
  }
```

Set up API Gateway: Create an **API Gateway** REST API to expose the Lambda function as an HTTP endpoint. Link the Lambda function to the API Gateway by setting the integration type to **Lambda Function**.
Steps:

- Go to API Gateway and create a new API.
- Create a new resource (e.g., /users), and a GET method to fetch user data by userID.
- In the method settings, choose **Lambda Function** as the integration type and select the Lambda function you created.

Deploy the API: Deploy the API to a new stage (e.g., prod). You will receive an endpoint URL to interact with your API. This URL will allow clients to send HTTP requests to your Lambda-backed DynamoDB service.
Example:
php-template
Copy

```
https://<api-id>.execute-api.<region>.amazonaws.com/prod/users/{userID}
```

Test the Serverless API: You can now test the API by sending HTTP requests to the endpoint. For instance, a GET request to /users/123 will trigger the Lambda function and return data from DynamoDB for the user with userID = 123.

9.5 Continuous Integration and Deployment for Cloud-Based APIs

Continuous Integration (CI) and Continuous Deployment (CD) are essential practices for maintaining high-quality software development processes, especially when deploying cloud-based APIs. CI/CD ensures that code changes are automatically tested, built, and deployed to production with minimal manual intervention, leading to faster releases and more reliable applications.

9.5.1 What is CI/CD?

- **Continuous Integration (CI)**: CI is the practice of automatically integrating code changes into a shared repository frequently (often multiple times a day). This practice helps catch bugs early and ensures that new code does not break the application.
- **Continuous Deployment (CD)**: CD refers to the automated process of deploying new versions of your application to production after they pass tests and quality checks. It ensures that new features and fixes are delivered to users quickly and reliably.

9.5.2 Setting Up CI/CD for Serverless APIs on AWS

AWS offers several tools to implement CI/CD for serverless APIs, such as **AWS CodePipeline**, **AWS CodeBuild**, and **AWS CodeDeploy**. These services integrate well with services like Lambda, DynamoDB, and API Gateway, enabling automated deployment of serverless applications.

Step 1: Set Up AWS CodeCommit (Source Repository)

1. **Create a Repository**: Create a Git-based repository in **AWS CodeCommit** or use **GitHub** for storing your Lambda function and API code.
2. **Commit Code**: Push your code changes to the repository. This will serve as the source for the CI/CD pipeline.

Step 2: Configure AWS CodeBuild (Build)
Create a Build Project: AWS **CodeBuild** will automatically build the Lambda function from the source code. Create a new build project and configure it to use your source repository.

Example buildspec.yml (defines the build process):
yaml
Copy
```
version: 0.2
phases:
  install:
    commands:
      - echo Installing dependencies...
      - pip install -r requirements.txt
  build:
    commands:
      - echo Build started on `date`
      - zip -r function.zip .
artifacts:
  files:
    - function.zip
```

Step 3: Set Up AWS CodePipeline (Pipeline)

1. **Create a Pipeline**: Use **AWS CodePipeline** to automate the entire process from commit to deployment. CodePipeline will orchestrate the flow of your CI/CD process, integrating with CodeCommit, CodeBuild, and Lambda.
2. **Define Stages**:
   - **Source Stage**: Connect to your CodeCommit or GitHub repository.
   - **Build Stage**: Integrate with AWS CodeBuild to package and test your Lambda function.
   - **Deploy Stage**: Set up the deployment process, which can trigger Lambda function updates or API Gateway deployment.

Step 4: Automate Deployment with AWS CodeDeploy

If you're using Lambda functions, **AWS CodeDeploy** can help automate the deployment of updated Lambda code. This includes handling traffic shifting, rollback on failure, and version management.

9.5.3 Monitoring CI/CD Pipelines

- Use **AWS CloudWatch** to monitor your CI/CD pipeline for errors or failures in the build or deployment process.

125

- Set up **alerts** to notify you when a failure occurs, ensuring that any issues are caught early in the process.

Chapter 10: Security for RESTful APIs

10.1 Securing Your API Endpoints

In today's digital world, ensuring that your RESTful APIs are secure is essential to protect sensitive data, prevent unauthorized access, and maintain the integrity of your application. Securing your API endpoints ensures that only authorized users and systems can interact with your data and services. This section will discuss several key strategies and best practices for securing your API endpoints.

10.1.1 Authentication

Authentication is the process of verifying the identity of a user or system making a request to your API. The goal of authentication is to ensure that only legitimate users or applications can access your API endpoints.

API Key Authentication

API keys are a simple form of authentication in which the client must provide a unique key when making requests. API keys are typically sent in the request header or as a query parameter. However, while API keys are easy to implement, they lack the advanced features required for handling sensitive data and should be used with caution.

Example of sending an API key in the request header:

```http
Copy
GET /user/profile HTTP/1.1
Host: api.example.com
API-Key: your-api-key-here
```

Pros:

- Easy to implement.
- Useful for rate-limiting and tracking API usage.

Cons:

- Lacks encryption (unless used with HTTPS).
- Static and vulnerable if exposed or leaked.

OAuth 2.0 Authentication

OAuth 2.0 is a more advanced and secure authentication method, often used to grant third-party applications limited access to an API. It allows users to authenticate via external providers (e.g., Google, Facebook, or an enterprise system) without sharing their credentials with the application.

OAuth 2.0 uses access tokens to authenticate users. The access token is passed in the Authorization header in the form of a **Bearer token**.

Example:

```
http
Copy
GET /user/profile HTTP/1.1
Host: api.example.com
Authorization: Bearer your-access-token-here
```

Pros:

- Highly secure and widely adopted.
- Supports user delegation for third-party access.
- Tokens can be scoped with specific access rights and expiration times.

Cons:

- More complex to implement.
- Requires token management infrastructure (e.g., refresh tokens).

JWT (JSON Web Token)

JWT is an open standard for securely transmitting information between parties as a JSON object. It is commonly used for authentication in RESTful APIs. JWT tokens are signed and optionally encrypted, allowing the API to verify the integrity of the data without requiring a database lookup.

A typical JWT contains three parts: header, payload, and signature. The payload contains user-specific data (e.g., user ID, roles), while the signature ensures that the payload is not tampered with.

Example of a JWT in the request header:

http
Copy
```
GET /user/profile HTTP/1.1
Host: api.example.com
Authorization: Bearer <your-jwt-token-here>
```

Pros:

- Stateless: The server does not need to store session information.
- Self-contained: Can store user data (e.g., roles, permissions) within the token.
- Compact and URL-safe.

Cons:

- Token management can become challenging.
- Token expiration and revocation need careful consideration.

10.1.2 Authorization

Once users are authenticated, the next step is **authorization**: determining whether a user has permission to access a particular resource or endpoint. Authorization is typically managed via **roles** and **permissions**, and it can be enforced using methods such as **Role-Based Access Control (RBAC)** or **Attribute-Based Access Control (ABAC)**.

Role-Based Access Control (RBAC)

In RBAC, access to resources is granted based on the user's role. Each role has specific permissions associated with it, and users are assigned one or more roles. This allows for simple and centralized access control management.

For example:

- **Admin**: Full access to all endpoints.
- **User**: Limited access to basic endpoints.
- **Guest**: Read-only access to public data.

Attribute-Based Access Control (ABAC)

ABAC is a more flexible approach where access is granted based on attributes such as user identity, location, time of access, or other context-specific data. ABAC can accommodate more granular control, especially in complex systems with multiple levels of access.

Access Control with API Gateway

You can leverage **AWS API Gateway** or similar tools to enforce authorization on API endpoints. API Gateway integrates with IAM (Identity and Access Management) policies or third-party authentication providers to ensure that only authorized users can access your resources.

10.1.3 Rate Limiting and Throttling

Rate limiting is another critical security measure that protects your API from abuse and denial-of-service (DoS) attacks. By limiting the number of requests a client can make in a given time frame, you can prevent overloads and mitigate the risk of malicious attacks.

- Use **API Gateway** to define rate limits.
- Implement **backoff strategies** (e.g., exponential backoff) to control request retries.
- Set **IP-based rate limits** or **user-based rate limits** depending on your application.

Example:

```http
Copy
HTTP/1.1 429 Too Many Requests
Retry-After: 60
```

10.1.4 Logging and Auditing

Ensuring that you have detailed logs of API access is essential for both security and debugging. You should log key events such as successful and failed authentication attempts, access to sensitive endpoints, and errors.

Use tools like **AWS CloudWatch** or **ELK Stack (Elasticsearch, Logstash, Kibana)** to capture and analyze logs in real time. Auditing access patterns can help detect suspicious activity and potential security breaches.

10.2 Encrypting Data at Rest and In Transit

Data encryption is a fundamental part of securing your API. It ensures that sensitive data is protected both when stored (at rest) and when transmitted between clients and servers (in transit). Let's explore the best practices for encrypting data at rest and in transit in RESTful APIs.

10.2.1 Encrypting Data at Rest

Data at rest refers to any data that is stored on disk, such as in databases, file systems, or object storage. Protecting data at rest is essential for ensuring that sensitive data remains secure, even if a storage device is compromised.

Encryption at the File System Level

At the file system level, many cloud providers offer **encryption-at-rest** by default for storage services like Amazon S3, RDS, and DynamoDB. When using cloud services, data is automatically encrypted using strong encryption algorithms (e.g., AES-256).

1. **Amazon RDS for PostgreSQL**: RDS provides **encryption at rest** for databases using the **AWS KMS (Key Management Service)** to manage the encryption keys.
2. **Amazon DynamoDB**: DynamoDB also automatically encrypts all data stored in tables, using AWS-managed keys.

Encryption at the Application Level

In some cases, you may need to handle encryption at the application level for more control over encryption keys. For example, you may want to encrypt sensitive fields (e.g., user passwords, financial data) before storing them in the database.

- **AES (Advanced Encryption Standard)** is commonly used for encrypting data at rest.
- **RSA** is another common encryption algorithm, used for public-key cryptography.

131

Here is an example of encrypting data before storing it in PostgreSQL using Python and **cryptography** library:

```python
Copy
from cryptography.fernet import Fernet

# Generate a key
key = Fernet.generate_key()
cipher_suite = Fernet(key)

# Encrypt data
encrypted_data = cipher_suite.encrypt(b"My sensitive data")

# Decrypt data
decrypted_data = cipher_suite.decrypt(encrypted_data)
```

Backup Encryption

Don't forget to encrypt your backups. RDS and DynamoDB provide backup encryption, but if you're managing your own backups, use encryption tools like **Amazon S3 server-side encryption** to ensure that backups are also protected.

10.2.2 Encrypting Data In Transit

Data in transit refers to any data that is being transmitted over the network. Encrypting data in transit ensures that it remains secure during transmission, preventing interception or tampering by unauthorized parties.

TLS/SSL Encryption

TLS (Transport Layer Security), the successor to SSL (Secure Sockets Layer), is the most widely used protocol for encrypting data in transit. When you use HTTPS (HTTP over SSL/TLS), the connection between the client and server is encrypted, making it secure against man-in-the-middle (MITM) attacks.

- Ensure that all API endpoints are accessed over **HTTPS**.
- Use **SSL/TLS certificates** from trusted certificate authorities (CAs), such as **Let's Encrypt** or **AWS ACM (AWS Certificate Manager)**.

Example of securing API communication using HTTPS:

http
Copy
```
GET /users/123 HTTP/1.1
Host: api.example.com
Authorization: Bearer <JWT-token>
```

Securing API Communication with OAuth 2.0 and JWT

In addition to encrypting data, securing API endpoints with **OAuth 2.0** or **JWT** adds an extra layer of security by ensuring that only authorized clients can access the API.

- Use **OAuth 2.0** with **Authorization Code Flow** or **Client Credentials Flow** to secure API endpoints.
- **JWT tokens** should be transmitted securely over HTTPS to ensure the confidentiality and integrity of the data.

Best Practices for Securing API Communication

- **Always use HTTPS**: Ensure that your API only accepts requests over HTTPS to protect data during transmission.
- **Use HSTS (HTTP Strict Transport Security)**: HSTS forces clients to communicate only over HTTPS, protecting against SSL stripping attacks.
- **Validate Certificates**: Validate SSL/TLS certificates to prevent man-in-the-middle attacks, and ensure that they are up-to-date and trusted by a recognized CA.

10.3 Protecting Against SQL Injection and NoSQL Injection

SQL Injection and **NoSQL Injection** are common attack vectors where malicious users inject harmful code into queries, allowing them to manipulate or access sensitive data. These types of attacks are prevalent in both relational databases (SQL) and NoSQL databases like DynamoDB, and both need to be carefully mitigated.

10.3.1 SQL Injection Attacks

SQL injection occurs when an attacker inserts or manipulates malicious SQL code within an application's query. This can allow the attacker to view, modify, or delete data, potentially compromising the entire database.

How SQL Injection Works

SQL injection typically exploits improperly sanitized user input. For example, consider a simple SQL query to retrieve a user's data by their username:

```sql
Copy
SELECT * FROM users WHERE username = '<user_input>';
```

If the input is not sanitized, an attacker could inject malicious code into the query:

```sql
Copy
SELECT * FROM users WHERE username = 'admin' OR '1'='1';
```

This would cause the query to always return data for the user "admin" because the condition '1'='1' is always true.

Protecting Against SQL Injection

Use Prepared Statements (Parameterized Queries): One of the most effective ways to protect against SQL injection is by using **prepared statements**. These statements bind user inputs as parameters rather than directly embedding them into the query. This ensures that user input is treated as data and not executable code.

Example (Python with psycopg2):

```python
Copy
cursor.execute("SELECT * FROM users WHERE username = %s", (username,))
```

1.
2. **Use ORM (Object-Relational Mapping) Tools**: Many web frameworks and libraries use ORMs (like Django ORM, SQLAlchemy, or Hibernate) to automatically generate SQL queries. These tools usually handle parameterized queries and protect against injection attacks.
3. **Input Validation**: Ensure that all user input is validated and sanitized before being used in a query. For instance, restrict usernames to alphanumeric characters and ensure that inputs conform to expected formats.
4. **Least Privilege Principle**: Use **least privilege** when configuring database access. Ensure that database accounts only have the permissions necessary for

their specific functions. This minimizes the potential impact of a successful injection attack.

10.3.2 NoSQL Injection Attacks

NoSQL injection attacks occur in non-relational databases (like MongoDB, Couchbase, and DynamoDB) when an attacker manipulates query parameters to execute malicious operations on the database.

How NoSQL Injection Works

In NoSQL databases, queries are often formed by embedding user input into query syntax. In a MongoDB query, for example, an attacker might inject a malicious query to bypass authentication or retrieve unauthorized data:

```javascript
Copy
db.users.find({ username: "admin" , password: "" OR 1=1 });
```

This query might return data for all users because the OR 1=1 condition is always true.

Protecting Against NoSQL Injection

1. **Use Parameterized Queries**: Just like SQL, ensure that NoSQL databases use parameterized queries or proper query-building methods that avoid directly inserting user input into the query string.
2. **Sanitize User Input**: Sanitize all user inputs by validating that they match the expected data types and formats. For example, ensuring that username is a string without any special characters can help prevent injections.
3. **Limit Query Capabilities**: Limit the power of queries by avoiding direct access to powerful operations like $eval in MongoDB or similar. Restrict operations that could modify the database unintentionally.
4. **Use Permissions and Access Controls**: Enforce strict access control and role-based permissions in your NoSQL database. Ensure that users and applications only have access to the data and operations they need.

10.4 Rate Limiting and Throttling to Prevent Abuse

Rate limiting and throttling are crucial for protecting APIs from abuse, ensuring that no user or application can overwhelm the system with excessive requests. These techniques help maintain service availability and ensure fair usage of API resources.

10.4.1 What is Rate Limiting?

Rate limiting is the process of limiting the number of requests a client can make to an API within a specified time period. It prevents excessive use of API resources and protects against malicious attacks like **Denial of Service (DoS)**.

How Rate Limiting Works

Rate limiting is usually implemented by keeping track of the number of requests made by a client in a given time window. If the number of requests exceeds a predefined threshold, the client is blocked or throttled.

Example of rate limiting:

- A client is allowed up to **1000 requests per hour**.
- Once the limit is reached, the client receives a **429 Too Many Requests** status code.

10.4.2 Throttling

Throttling is similar to rate limiting, but it typically refers to slowing down the request processing rather than blocking it entirely. Throttling is used to control the pace of requests to prevent a service from being overwhelmed while still allowing clients to continue making requests at a slower rate.

How Throttling Works

When throttling is applied, the system might:

- **Queue** requests and process them later.
- **Delay** responses with a **Retry-After** header to indicate when the client should try again.

Example:

http
Copy
HTTP/1.1 429 Too Many Requests
Retry-After: 60

10.4.3 Implementing Rate Limiting and Throttling

1. **API Gateway and Lambda**: In AWS, **API Gateway** can be configured to implement rate limiting for API endpoints. You can set **throttle settings** at both the global level (for all APIs) and the resource level (for specific APIs). API Gateway supports burst limits and steady-state limits to handle sudden traffic spikes without overwhelming the backend.
2. **Leverage Redis for Request Tracking**: Use tools like **Redis** or **Memcached** to track request counts in real-time. These in-memory data stores are fast and efficient for tracking API usage within a short time period.
3. **Custom Rate Limiting Logic**: Implement custom rate limiting logic using application code if you're building your own API gateway or proxy. This typically involves checking the IP address or API key of the incoming request, tracking the number of requests, and enforcing limits.

Example of rate-limiting logic in Python using Flask:

python
Copy
```
from flask import Flask, request, jsonify
from time import time

app = Flask(__name__)

# Store timestamps of requests per user
requests = {}

@app.route('/api', methods=['GET'])
def api():
    user_ip = request.remote_addr
    current_time = time()
```

137

```
# Limit requests to 100 per minute
if user_ip not in requests:
    requests[user_ip] = []

# Clean up outdated requests
requests[user_ip] = [timestamp for timestamp in requests[user_ip] if current_time -
timestamp < 60]

# Check if the user exceeds the rate limit
if len(requests[user_ip]) >= 100:
    return jsonify({"message": "Rate limit exceeded"}), 429

# Allow the request and store the timestamp
requests[user_ip].append(current_time)
return jsonify({"message": "Request accepted"})

if __name__ == '__main__':
    app.run()
```

10.4.4 Best Practices for Rate Limiting and Throttling

1. **Define Clear Limits**: Define reasonable limits based on your API's use case. For example, an API providing public data might have higher limits than an API providing sensitive data.
2. **Use Sliding Windows**: Instead of resetting the count at fixed intervals (e.g., every minute), use a **sliding window** to calculate rate limits based on actual requests.
3. **Return Retry-After Header**: When a user hits the rate limit, return the Retry-After header with the time in seconds when the user can retry the request.
4. **Differentiate by User or IP**: Implement rate limits based on the user's API key, IP address, or account to ensure fairness in usage.

10.5 Using AWS IAM and PostgreSQL Security Best Practices

Security is essential when deploying PostgreSQL in cloud environments, particularly when using cloud platforms like **AWS**. AWS **Identity and Access Management (IAM)** plays a significant role in securing your PostgreSQL databases and API interactions.

138

Additionally, PostgreSQL itself offers several best practices to ensure that your database is secure from unauthorized access.

10.5.1 AWS IAM Security Best Practices

AWS IAM enables you to securely control access to AWS resources, including RDS instances, Lambda functions, and API Gateway. When integrating PostgreSQL with AWS, IAM policies help ensure that only authorized users and services have access to your database and other resources.

Key IAM Best Practices:

1. **Use Least Privilege**: Always follow the **least privilege** principle by granting the minimum permissions necessary for the task at hand. Avoid using the root account for everyday tasks and create IAM roles with specific policies for different resources.
2. **Use IAM Roles for EC2 Instances and Lambda Functions**: Attach IAM roles to your **EC2 instances** or **Lambda functions** that need access to the RDS PostgreSQL database. This eliminates the need to hardcode database credentials into your application.
3. **Enable Multi-Factor Authentication (MFA)**: Enable MFA for IAM users with access to sensitive AWS resources, including RDS instances. MFA adds an extra layer of protection to your AWS account.
4. **Use IAM Policies for Fine-Grained Access Control**: For PostgreSQL instances hosted in **Amazon RDS**, you can control access by applying IAM policies. For example, you can create policies that specify which IAM users or roles can manage PostgreSQL databases, perform backups, or modify configurations.

Example of an IAM policy allowing access to RDS:

json
Copy
```
{
  "Version": "2012-10-17",
  "Statement": [
    {
      "Effect": "Allow",
      "Action": "rds:DescribeDBInstances",
      "Resource": "*"
    }
```

```
    ]
}
```

10.5.2 PostgreSQL Security Best Practices

When securing PostgreSQL itself, there are several practices you should follow to ensure that your database is properly protected from unauthorized access and attacks.

1. **Use Strong Passwords**: Use strong passwords for PostgreSQL superuser roles and application users. Enforce password complexity requirements to ensure that weak passwords are not used.

Enable SSL/TLS: Always use **SSL/TLS** encryption for client-server communication. This ensures that data is encrypted in transit, protecting it from man-in-the-middle (MITM) attacks. You can configure PostgreSQL to require SSL for all connections by modifying the postgresql.conf file.
Example:
ini
Copy
ssl = on

2.
3. **Limit User Permissions**: Only grant permissions necessary for the user to perform their tasks. Use **role-based access control** (RBAC) in PostgreSQL to manage access at the user and group levels. Avoid granting superuser privileges unless absolutely necessary.
4. **Regularly Update PostgreSQL**: Regularly apply patches and updates to PostgreSQL to protect against known vulnerabilities. Enable **automatic updates** where possible, or regularly check for new releases and security patches.
5. **Use Network Firewalls**: Limit access to PostgreSQL instances by restricting inbound traffic using **firewalls** or **Security Groups** in AWS. Only allow trusted IP addresses or VPCs to access the database.

Chapter 11: Error Handling, Logging, and Monitoring

11.1 Structuring Error Responses in RESTful APIs

Error handling is a critical part of building resilient and user-friendly RESTful APIs. How errors are reported to the client can significantly affect both the debugging process and the user experience. Well-structured error responses provide clear feedback to clients and help ensure that the API behaves predictably, even in the face of failure.

In this section, we'll discuss best practices for structuring error responses, including the importance of standardized error formats, using appropriate HTTP status codes, and providing useful error details.

11.1.1 The Importance of Standardizing Error Responses

Consistency in error handling is crucial for API consumers, who often rely on a standardized approach to handle failures efficiently. By using a consistent error structure, you provide clients with a predictable format for handling different types of errors, leading to better user experiences and easier troubleshooting.

A standardized error response should contain:

- **HTTP Status Code**: The HTTP status code indicates the outcome of the request (e.g., success, client error, or server error).
- **Error Code**: An internal error code to categorize the error and help both developers and API consumers understand the problem.
- **Error Message**: A human-readable message that explains the nature of the error.
- **Details**: Optional details that can provide more context (e.g., specific validation failures, missing parameters, or internal error logs).
- **Timestamp**: The time when the error occurred, which can be helpful for debugging issues in real-time.

A consistent error response format makes it easy for clients to process and handle errors programmatically. Below is an example of a well-structured error response:

11.1.2 Example of a Standardized Error Response Format

json

Copy

```json
{
  "status": "error",
  "message": "Invalid request parameters",
  "error_code": "400_BAD_REQUEST",
  "details": {
    "missing_field": "email",
    "invalid_field": "age"
  },
  "timestamp": "2025-02-12T14:35:00Z"
}
```

- **status**: Indicates the status of the response (e.g., success or error).
- **message**: Provides a short, human-readable explanation of the error.
- **error_code**: A predefined internal code that categorizes the error (this helps both developers and automated systems).
- **details**: A more detailed explanation of the error. In this case, it explains which fields are missing or invalid.
- **timestamp**: Provides the exact time of the error for logging and troubleshooting purposes.

11.1.3 Using Appropriate HTTP Status Codes

The **HTTP status code** communicates the general outcome of the request. Proper use of status codes enables clients to easily categorize errors and decide how to proceed. Below are common HTTP status codes used for error handling:

- **400 Bad Request**: The request was malformed or missing required parameters. This is commonly used for validation errors.
- **401 Unauthorized**: The request lacks valid authentication credentials.
- **403 Forbidden**: The request is valid but the user does not have permission to access the resource.
- **404 Not Found**: The requested resource does not exist.
- **422 Unprocessable Entity**: The server understands the request, but the request data is semantically incorrect or invalid (often used for validation errors).
- **500 Internal Server Error**: The server encountered an unexpected condition that prevented it from fulfilling the request.

11.1.4 Error Handling for Different Scenarios

Validation Errors: When users provide invalid data, such as a missing required field or an invalid email format, return a 400 Bad Request or 422 Unprocessable Entity status code with a detailed message indicating the issue with the request.

Example:

json

Copy

```
{
  "status": "error",
  "message": "Validation error",
  "error_code": "400_BAD_REQUEST",
  "details": {
    "missing_field": "username"
  },
  "timestamp": "2025-02-12T14:40:00Z"
}
```

Authentication and Authorization Errors: For unauthorized or forbidden access, use 401 Unauthorized or 403 Forbidden, and provide an error message that guides the user to authenticate or gain the necessary permissions.

Example:

json

Copy

```
{
  "status": "error",
  "message": "Authentication failed",
  "error_code": "401_UNAUTHORIZED",
  "timestamp": "2025-02-12T14:45:00Z"
}
```

Internal Server Errors: For unexpected issues on the server, return 500 Internal Server Error. While the specific cause may not always be available, consider logging the issue in detail and providing a generic message for the client.

Example:
json
Copy

```
{
 "status": "error",
 "message": "An unexpected error occurred. Please try again later.",
 "error_code": "500_INTERNAL_SERVER_ERROR",
 "timestamp": "2025-02-12T14:50:00Z"
}
```

•

11.1.5 Client Error vs. Server Error

It's important to distinguish between **client errors** (4xx status codes) and **server errors** (5xx status codes):

- **Client Errors (4xx)**: These indicate that the problem lies with the client, such as invalid input, unauthorized access, or missing parameters.
- **Server Errors (5xx)**: These indicate problems with the server, such as failures in processing requests, database issues, or service outages.

Properly categorizing the error helps clients handle failures appropriately. For instance, a 401 Unauthorized error requires the client to authenticate, while a 500 Internal Server Error might trigger a retry mechanism or alert the development team.

11.2 Best Practices for Logging and Monitoring

Effective **logging** and **monitoring** are essential for maintaining the health of your API and ensuring that any issues are detected and resolved quickly. Logs provide valuable insights into the API's performance, usage, and potential errors, while monitoring ensures that you are alerted to anomalies or failures in real-time.

11.2.1 Logging Best Practices

Logs are a powerful tool for troubleshooting and performance analysis, but they need to be structured, secure, and meaningful. Here are some key practices to follow when implementing logging for your RESTful APIs:

1. Log in JSON Format

Structured logging in **JSON** format allows for easier parsing and analysis. Each log entry should contain relevant fields such as:

- **timestamp**: The exact time of the log entry.
- **level**: The severity of the log entry (e.g., INFO, WARN, ERROR, DEBUG).
- **message**: A brief description of the event.
- **context**: Additional contextual information, such as user ID, request ID, or endpoint accessed.

Example:

json
Copy

```json
{
  "timestamp": "2025-02-12T14:55:00Z",
  "level": "ERROR",
  "message": "Failed to process user request",
  "context": {
    "user_id": "12345",
    "request_id": "abcd1234",
    "error_details": "Missing required field 'email'"
  }
}
```

2. Use Appropriate Log Levels

Log levels help categorize the importance of the logs:

- **DEBUG**: Used for detailed debugging information.
- **INFO**: For general, operational messages such as successful API calls.
- **WARN**: For potential issues that do not interrupt the normal functioning of the application but might need attention.

- **ERROR**: For failures, exceptions, or critical issues that require immediate attention.
- **FATAL**: For severe errors that cause the application to stop functioning.

3. Log Essential Information

Ensure that your logs capture all necessary details, such as:

- **Request and response details**: Log incoming requests and responses, including headers, parameters, and response status codes. Be mindful of sensitive data—avoid logging private information like passwords, authentication tokens, or personal data.
- **Error stack traces**: When an error occurs, log the full stack trace along with contextual information to help developers trace the source of the issue.
- **Request IDs**: Use **request IDs** (unique identifiers for each request) to help trace errors across systems and services.

4. Log Rotation and Retention

Logs can grow quickly, so it's important to configure **log rotation** to archive old logs and keep the log files from becoming too large. Set up a **retention policy** to automatically delete logs after a certain period, keeping your storage costs manageable while maintaining enough data for analysis.

5. Ensure Secure Logging

Make sure that sensitive data, such as user credentials or payment information, is not logged. Use **redaction** to sanitize sensitive details before logging. Additionally, ensure that access to logs is restricted to authorized personnel only to prevent unauthorized access to sensitive information.

11.2.2 Monitoring Best Practices

Monitoring your RESTful API helps ensure that the system is healthy and that you are alerted to any issues before they impact users. By leveraging **monitoring tools** and setting up proactive alerting, you can track API performance, detect anomalies, and quickly respond to issues.

1. Monitor Key Metrics

Track essential metrics to assess the health and performance of your API:

- **Response Time**: Monitor the average time it takes for your API to respond to requests. A significant increase in response time could indicate a performance bottleneck.
- **Request Volume**: Track the total number of requests your API receives, and identify peak traffic periods.
- **Error Rate**: Keep an eye on the rate of errors (e.g., 4xx and 5xx status codes). A spike in error rates may point to issues with the API, such as increased client errors or backend failures.
- **Latency**: Measure the time taken for requests to travel between the client and the server, as well as any intermediate layers such as API Gateway or load balancers.

2. Use Distributed Tracing

Distributed tracing allows you to track requests across multiple services or microservices, providing visibility into the end-to-end journey of a request. Tools like **AWS X-Ray** or **Jaeger** allow you to trace individual requests as they pass through various systems, helping you identify performance bottlenecks and failures.

3. Set Up Alerts

Proactively monitor your API with **CloudWatch Alarms** or third-party monitoring tools like **Datadog** or **New Relic**. Set up alerts for abnormal behavior, such as:

- Increased error rates
- Slow response times
- High resource utilization (e.g., CPU, memory, or database performance)

For example, you could set an alarm that triggers when the error rate exceeds a specific threshold, allowing your team to investigate the issue before it affects users.

4. Analyze Logs in Real-Time

Integrate your logs with real-time log analysis tools like **AWS CloudWatch Logs**, **Elasticsearch**, or **Splunk**. These tools help you quickly identify issues, such as unusual spikes in errors or performance degradation, by analyzing log data in real time.

5. Automated Incident Response

Automate incident response processes by integrating monitoring tools with incident management systems (e.g., **PagerDuty** or **Opsgenie**). When an alert is triggered, these tools can automatically notify the relevant team members and create an incident ticket to ensure a timely response.

11.3 Using AWS CloudWatch for DynamoDB Logs

AWS CloudWatch is a powerful tool that provides monitoring and observability for AWS services, including **DynamoDB**. CloudWatch allows you to collect, monitor, and analyze logs in real-time, providing valuable insights into the performance of your DynamoDB tables. In this section, we will explore how to leverage CloudWatch for logging and monitoring DynamoDB operations.

11.3.1 DynamoDB Streams and CloudWatch Integration

DynamoDB Streams capture changes to items in your DynamoDB tables, enabling you to track and log changes made to data. By integrating DynamoDB Streams with **AWS CloudWatch Logs**, you can create a system that automatically sends change data from DynamoDB to CloudWatch for further analysis.

Setting up DynamoDB Streams

1. **Enable DynamoDB Streams**: When creating or updating a DynamoDB table, enable **DynamoDB Streams** to capture item-level changes (INSERT, MODIFY, REMOVE).
2. **Choose Stream View Type**: Select the stream view type that best fits your use case. Common options are:
   - **NEW_IMAGE**: Captures the entire item after the change.
   - **OLD_IMAGE**: Captures the item before the change.
   - **NEW_AND_OLD_IMAGES**: Captures both the item before and after the change.

Integrating DynamoDB Streams with CloudWatch

Create a Lambda Function: Write an AWS Lambda function to process DynamoDB Streams and send log data to CloudWatch. This Lambda function can filter the stream data and create custom log entries in CloudWatch.

Example Lambda function:
python
Copy

```python
import json
import boto3
from datetime import datetime

cloudwatch = boto3.client('logs')

def lambda_handler(event, context):
    for record in event['Records']:
        # Extract the change information from the record
        change = record['dynamodb']
        timestamp = datetime.now().isoformat()

        # Create a CloudWatch log entry
        log_message = {
            "timestamp": timestamp,
            "change": change
        }

        # Send the log data to CloudWatch
        cloudwatch.put_log_events(
            logGroupName='/aws/dynamodb/changes',
            logStreamName='stream1',
            logEvents=[{
                'timestamp': int(datetime.now().timestamp() * 1000),
                'message': json.dumps(log_message)
            }]
        )

    return {'statusCode': 200, 'body': 'Success'}
```

1. **Create CloudWatch Log Group**: In the AWS Console, create a **CloudWatch Log Group** and define a log stream (e.g., /aws/dynamodb/changes) to store the DynamoDB stream logs.
2. **Monitor DynamoDB Performance**: Once the integration is complete, you can monitor the logs in **CloudWatch Logs** to track DynamoDB activity. Use

CloudWatch dashboards to visualize logs and set up alerts for important events (e.g., high read/write capacity usage, table throttling, etc.).

11.3.2 DynamoDB Metrics in CloudWatch

AWS CloudWatch also collects a set of **DynamoDB-specific metrics** that can be monitored to track performance and usage. These include metrics for read and write throughput, latency, and errors. Some of the important DynamoDB metrics available in CloudWatch include:

- **ConsumedReadCapacityUnits**: Tracks the number of read capacity units consumed.
- **ConsumedWriteCapacityUnits**: Tracks the number of write capacity units consumed.
- **ThrottledRequests**: Indicates how many requests were throttled due to exceeding the provisioned capacity.
- **SystemErrors**: Tracks errors generated by DynamoDB operations.

These metrics can be used to set up CloudWatch alarms, ensuring that you are alerted whenever DynamoDB starts to experience problems, such as high latency or throttling.

11.4 Analyzing PostgreSQL Logs for Performance and Errors

PostgreSQL provides several log files that can be used to track and analyze performance, identify errors, and optimize queries. By properly configuring PostgreSQL logging, you can monitor critical aspects such as slow queries, deadlocks, connection issues, and system errors.

11.4.1 Enabling PostgreSQL Logging

PostgreSQL logs can be enabled and configured in the **postgresql.conf** file. Some key parameters for logging include:

1. **log_statement**: Determines which types of SQL statements are logged. You can choose between logging all statements, only failed ones, or only specific types of queries (e.g., SELECT, INSERT).

Set to all to log all statements:
ini
Copy
log_statement = 'all'

- Set to mod for logging only modification queries (e.g., INSERT, UPDATE, DELETE).

log_duration: Logs the duration of each SQL statement. Setting this to on will log the time taken for each query.
ini
Copy
log_duration = on

log_min_duration_statement: Logs queries that exceed a specified execution time (in milliseconds). This is useful for identifying slow queries that may need optimization.
ini
Copy
log_min_duration_statement = 1000 # Log queries that take longer than 1000ms

log_error_verbosity: Defines the verbosity of error messages. Options are terse, default, and verbose.
ini
Copy
log_error_verbosity = 'default'

log_line_prefix: Controls the format of the log entry. This can include elements like the time of the query, the user running the query, and the database name.
ini
Copy
log_line_prefix = '%t [%p]: [%l-1] user=%u,db=%d,app=%a '

After making changes to postgresql.conf, reload the PostgreSQL service to apply the new logging settings:

bash
Copy
SELECT pg_reload_conf();

11.4.2 Key Logs to Monitor

- **Slow Queries**: Slow query logs help you identify queries that take longer than expected to execute. These queries can be optimized by analyzing their execution plans and adjusting indexing strategies.
- **Deadlocks**: PostgreSQL logs deadlock errors when two or more transactions block each other. Identifying deadlocks can help you understand the root cause of the issue and take corrective actions, such as adjusting transaction isolation levels or refactoring the application logic.

Example of a deadlock log entry:

text
Copy
ERROR: deadlock detected
DETAIL: Process 1234 waits for ShareLock on transaction 5678; blocked by process 2345.

- **Connection Issues**: PostgreSQL logs errors when there are connection problems, such as failing to establish a connection or exceeding the maximum allowed connections. These logs can help identify resource issues, such as insufficient system resources or a need to scale up the PostgreSQL instance.

11.4.3 Analyzing PostgreSQL Logs with External Tools

Once logs are generated, they can be analyzed for trends and patterns. Use external tools like **pgBadger** or **pgFouine** to analyze PostgreSQL logs. These tools provide detailed reports and visualizations of slow queries, error rates, and performance bottlenecks.

pgBadger: pgBadger is a fast and feature-rich log analyzer for PostgreSQL that parses log files and generates detailed reports in HTML, JSON, or CSV format. You can use it to visualize query performance, check for query bottlenecks, and review system logs.

Example command to generate a report:
bash
Copy
pgbadger -f stderr /var/log/postgresql/postgresql.log

-

11.4.4 PostgreSQL Performance Tuning

PostgreSQL logs also provide insights into performance issues, such as resource bottlenecks or inefficient queries. By analyzing query performance in the logs, you can:

- **Optimize slow queries** by adding indexes, rewriting queries, or adjusting query plans.
- **Tune PostgreSQL parameters** like work_mem, shared_buffers, and effective_cache_size based on the observed performance.
- **Adjust the autovacuum settings** to ensure that database maintenance tasks (such as vacuuming dead tuples) run efficiently without affecting performance.

11.5 Real-Time Monitoring Tools and Dashboards

Real-time monitoring is crucial for maintaining the health and performance of your APIs and databases. It allows you to detect issues early, monitor system performance, and ensure your application is running smoothly.

11.5.1 AWS CloudWatch for Real-Time Monitoring

AWS CloudWatch is a robust monitoring tool that provides real-time insights into the performance and health of your AWS resources. It can be used to monitor both DynamoDB and PostgreSQL (via RDS or EC2) and track metrics such as resource utilization, request rates, error rates, and latency.

1. **Create CloudWatch Dashboards**: Use CloudWatch Dashboards to create custom views of your metrics. These dashboards can display key performance indicators (KPIs) such as database throughput, API latency, and error rates in a single pane of glass.
2. **Set Up CloudWatch Alarms**: CloudWatch Alarms can be configured to trigger actions based on specific conditions, such as high CPU utilization or increased error rates. Alarms can be used to send notifications via **SNS** (Simple

Notification Service) or trigger **Lambda functions** to remediate issues automatically.

Example of setting an alarm for high error rates:

bash
Copy
```
aws cloudwatch put-metric-alarm --alarm-name HighErrorRate --metric-name 4xxError
--namespace AWS/ApiGateway --statistic Sum --period 60 --threshold 100
--comparison-operator GreaterThanThreshold --evaluation-periods 1 --alarm-actions
arn:aws:sns:us-east-1:123456789012:NotifyMe
```

11.5.2 Datadog for Real-Time API Monitoring

Datadog is a powerful monitoring tool that provides detailed insights into the performance of your APIs, databases, and infrastructure. It integrates with both DynamoDB and PostgreSQL, offering advanced features like distributed tracing, log management, and customizable dashboards.

Datadog Features:

- **Real-time Dashboards**: Datadog offers real-time dashboards that allow you to visualize performance metrics such as latency, throughput, and error rates.
- **APM (Application Performance Monitoring)**: Datadog's APM provides detailed insights into how your APIs and databases are performing by tracing requests and transactions from end to end.
- **Log Management**: Datadog's log management tool allows you to aggregate and analyze logs from various sources, providing a comprehensive view of your system's health.

11.5.3 Prometheus and Grafana for Monitoring and Dashboards

Prometheus is an open-source monitoring tool designed for high-scale applications, while **Grafana** is used to visualize data stored in Prometheus (and other data sources). Together, they provide powerful capabilities for real-time monitoring and analysis of application performance.

1. **Prometheus Metrics Collection**: Prometheus collects data from various services, including PostgreSQL, by scraping endpoints that expose metrics in a

format that Prometheus can understand. Use the postgres_exporter to expose PostgreSQL metrics to Prometheus.

2. **Grafana Dashboards**: Grafana provides customizable dashboards for visualizing Prometheus metrics. You can create real-time dashboards to monitor PostgreSQL performance, such as query execution times, connection statistics, and database health.

Example: You can set up a **Grafana dashboard** to track the latency of your PostgreSQL queries, monitoring key metrics like query execution time, query count, and error rate.

Chapter 12: Advanced Topics: GraphQL APIs and Hybrid Architectures

12.1 Introduction to GraphQL

GraphQL is a modern query language for APIs that allows clients to request exactly the data they need and nothing more. It was developed by **Facebook** in 2012 and released as an open-source project in 2015. Unlike traditional RESTful APIs, where endpoints are tied to fixed data structures, GraphQL provides a flexible and efficient way to interact with your data, empowering clients to shape the responses to their specific needs.

12.1.1 What is GraphQL?

At its core, GraphQL provides a more efficient, powerful, and flexible alternative to REST APIs. It enables developers to query multiple resources in a single request, specify exactly what data they need, and even modify the structure of responses.

In a typical REST API, you might have several endpoints that return different types of data. For example, you could have endpoints like /users, /posts, and /comments, each returning different pieces of data. The downside to this approach is that clients often retrieve more data than they need, requiring additional requests and causing inefficiencies. GraphQL solves this problem by allowing clients to request only the fields they require from a single endpoint.

A GraphQL query looks like this:

```graphql
Copy
{
  users {
    name
    email
    posts {
      title
      body
    }
  }
}
```

This query will return a response like this:

```json
Copy
{
  "data": {
    "users": [
      {
        "name": "John Doe",
        "email": "john.doe@example.com",
        "posts": [
          {
            "title": "GraphQL is Awesome",
            "body": "GraphQL allows clients to request exactly the data they need."
          }
        ]
      }
    ]
  }
}
```

The flexibility in data retrieval allows clients to get the exact data they need in a single request, reducing the need for multiple HTTP calls, improving performance, and simplifying API interactions.

12.1.2 Key Features of GraphQL

1. **Declarative Data Fetching**: With GraphQL, clients specify what data they need, which reduces over-fetching and under-fetching of data. Instead of hitting multiple endpoints for different resources, a single query is sent to the server, and only the requested fields are returned.
2. **Strongly Typed Schema**: GraphQL APIs are schema-based, meaning the structure of the API is defined up front. The schema describes the types of data that can be queried and the relationships between them. It serves as both a contract and documentation for how the API should behave.
3. **Single Endpoint**: Unlike REST, which typically has multiple endpoints (e.g., /users, /posts, /comments), GraphQL operates on a single endpoint (usually /graphql). This simplifies the client-server interaction and reduces the complexity of managing multiple endpoints.

4. **Real-time Data with Subscriptions**: GraphQL allows for real-time updates through **subscriptions**. Clients can subscribe to changes in data, receiving automatic updates when data changes on the server, which is useful for applications that require real-time data updates, such as chat apps or live feeds.
5. **Introspection**: GraphQL APIs are self-documenting due to their introspective nature. Clients can query the API's schema to discover the types, fields, and operations available, making it easy for developers to explore and understand the API without external documentation.

12.1.3 Why Use GraphQL?

- **Reduced Over-fetching and Under-fetching**: GraphQL allows clients to fetch exactly the data they need, reducing unnecessary data transfer and improving efficiency.
- **Faster Development**: The flexibility of GraphQL allows frontend developers to work independently of backend developers, as they can query the server for any data they need without requiring changes to the backend API.
- **Strong Typing and Validation**: The strongly typed nature of GraphQL ensures that queries are validated before execution, making it easier to catch errors early.
- **Backend Aggregation**: GraphQL can aggregate data from multiple sources (such as databases, REST APIs, and microservices) into a single query, simplifying data retrieval from multiple sources.

12.2 Using GraphQL with DynamoDB

Integrating **GraphQL** with **DynamoDB** enables developers to build highly flexible, scalable, and efficient APIs. **DynamoDB** is a fully managed NoSQL database service from AWS that provides fast and predictable performance at any scale. When combined with GraphQL, DynamoDB can serve as a highly scalable backend for serving data with flexible querying capabilities, without the complexity of SQL joins or traditional relational schemas.

12.2.1 Why Use GraphQL with DynamoDB?

While **GraphQL** is known for its flexibility and ability to handle complex queries, **DynamoDB** provides a fast, scalable, and highly available database solution. Using DynamoDB as a backend for a GraphQL API has several advantages:

- **Scalability**: DynamoDB can scale automatically to accommodate any level of traffic, making it ideal for GraphQL APIs that may require the ability to handle a large number of concurrent requests.
- **Real-time Updates**: DynamoDB Streams can be used in conjunction with GraphQL subscriptions to provide real-time updates, where clients receive automatic updates when data in DynamoDB changes.
- **Flexibility**: GraphQL's schema-based querying allows you to define complex, flexible queries that interact with the unstructured, key-value store of DynamoDB, providing the best of both worlds.

12.2.2 Setting Up GraphQL with DynamoDB

To set up a GraphQL API with DynamoDB, we typically use **AWS AppSync**, a managed service that simplifies building GraphQL APIs by providing direct integration with DynamoDB. AppSync handles real-time data synchronization, offline access, and user authentication, and it supports DynamoDB as a primary data source.

Step 1: Setting Up DynamoDB

Before setting up the GraphQL API, you need to create your DynamoDB table.

1. **Create a DynamoDB Table**: In the AWS console, create a DynamoDB table to store your data. Let's say we create a Users table with userID as the partition key.

Insert Data into DynamoDB: Populate the DynamoDB table with sample data. For example:

json
Copy

```
{
  "userID": "1",
  "name": "John Doe",
  "email": "john.doe@example.com",
  "posts": [
    { "title": "GraphQL Basics", "body": "This is an introduction to GraphQL" },
```

{ "title": "DynamoDB with GraphQL", "body": "Integrating GraphQL with DynamoDB" }
    ]
}

Step 2: Create an AppSync GraphQL API

1. **Create a GraphQL API**: In the AWS AppSync console, create a new GraphQL API and define the schema that matches the structure of your DynamoDB table. For example:

```graphql
type Post {
  title: String
  body: String
}

type User {
  userID: ID!
  name: String
  email: String
  posts: [Post]
}

type Query {
  getUser(userID: ID!): User
}

schema {
  query: Query
}
```

2. **Connect to DynamoDB**: Once your API is created, you can add a **data source** for DynamoDB. AppSync will use the table you created earlier as a data source. This allows the API to fetch data from DynamoDB in response to queries.

Step 3: Resolver Mapping

Resolvers are used to connect GraphQL queries to data sources. In this case, we create resolvers to connect queries like getUser to DynamoDB operations.

Define a Resolver for the getUser Query: In AWS AppSync, configure a resolver for the getUser query to fetch the user from the DynamoDB table. You can do this using a **VTL (Velocity Template Language)** mapping template. For example:

vtl
Copy

```
{
  "version": "2017-02-28",
  "operation": "GetItem",
  "key": {
    "userID": $util.dynamodb.toDynamoDBJson($ctx.arguments.userID)
  }
}
```

This mapping tells AppSync to fetch the item from DynamoDB where the userID matches the userID argument provided in the query.

Step 4: Testing the API

Once everything is set up, you can test your GraphQL API by querying the API endpoint. Here's an example query to retrieve a user and their posts:

graphql
Copy

```
{
  getUser(userID: "1") {
    name
    email
    posts {
      title
      body
    }
  }
}
```

The response might look like this:

json
Copy
```
{
 "data": {
  "getUser": {
   "name": "John Doe",
   "email": "john.doe@example.com",
   "posts": [
     { "title": "GraphQL Basics", "body": "This is an introduction to GraphQL" },
     { "title": "DynamoDB with GraphQL", "body": "Integrating GraphQL with
DynamoDB" }
   ]
  }
 }
}
```

12.2.3 Optimizing GraphQL Queries with DynamoDB

While GraphQL allows you to specify exactly what data you want, it's important to keep
DynamoDB's limitations and best practices in mind when designing the API:

1. **Efficient Querying**: DynamoDB is optimized for fast lookups based on a
   primary key or secondary index. To optimize queries, ensure your GraphQL API
   makes use of DynamoDB's indexed attributes for quick lookups. Avoid scanning
   entire tables whenever possible.
2. **Batch Operations**: DynamoDB supports **batch reads** and **batch writes**, which
   can improve the performance of your GraphQL API when multiple related items
   need to be fetched or updated simultaneously.
3. **Pagination**: For large datasets, implement **pagination** in your GraphQL queries
   to avoid overloading your DynamoDB table with large scans or queries that
   return too much data at once. GraphQL provides built-in support for paginated
   responses.

162

Example:

```graphql
Copy
{
  getUser(userID: "1") {
    name
    posts(limit: 10, nextToken: "xyz") {
      title
      body
    }
  }
}
```

4. **Caching**: Leverage caching mechanisms (e.g., **AWS AppSync's built-in caching**) to reduce the load on DynamoDB and improve response times for frequently requested data.

12.3 Using GraphQL with PostgreSQL

Integrating **GraphQL** with **PostgreSQL** allows you to leverage the power of a relational database while taking advantage of the flexibility and efficiency of GraphQL. PostgreSQL, known for its powerful query capabilities, joins, and transaction management, pairs well with GraphQL to expose relational data in a flexible, user-friendly way. By using GraphQL with PostgreSQL, you can create APIs that provide clients with exactly the data they need, eliminating over-fetching and under-fetching issues.

12.3.1 Setting Up a GraphQL API with PostgreSQL

To integrate GraphQL with PostgreSQL, you can use **Node.js** or frameworks like **Apollo Server** to build a GraphQL API, while connecting it to a PostgreSQL database for querying data. Below are the steps for setting up a simple GraphQL API with PostgreSQL.

Step 1: Setting Up PostgreSQL

First, ensure that PostgreSQL is properly set up and populated with some data. For instance, create a users table with the following structure:

sql
Copy
```
CREATE TABLE users (
    id SERIAL PRIMARY KEY,
    name VARCHAR(100),
    email VARCHAR(100) UNIQUE NOT NULL,
    created_at TIMESTAMP DEFAULT CURRENT_TIMESTAMP
);
```

Populate the table with sample data:

sql
Copy
```
INSERT INTO users (name, email) VALUES
('John Doe', 'john.doe@example.com'),
('Jane Smith', 'jane.smith@example.com');
```

Step 2: Setting Up Apollo Server with PostgreSQL

Apollo Server is a popular library for building GraphQL APIs. To use it with PostgreSQL, follow these steps:

1. **Install Dependencies**:
   - apollo-server for GraphQL server
   - pg for PostgreSQL client
   - graphql for GraphQL schema definitions

Example using npm:
bash
Copy
```
npm install apollo-server pg graphql
```

2. Create the GraphQL Schema: Define the types and queries for interacting with the PostgreSQL data. Here's an example of a GraphQL schema that queries users:
graphql
Copy

```graphql
type User {
  id: ID!
  name: String!
  email: String!
  created_at: String!
}

type Query {
  getUser(id: ID!): User
  getUsers: [User]
}
```

3. Define the Resolvers: Resolvers are functions that handle the logic of fetching data for each field in the GraphQL schema. In this case, the resolvers will interact with the PostgreSQL database.
javascript
Copy

```javascript
const { ApolloServer, gql } = require('apollo-server');
const { Client } = require('pg');

// Define GraphQL schema
const typeDefs = gql`
  type User {
    id: ID!
    name: String!
    email: String!
    created_at: String!
  }

  type Query {
    getUser(id: ID!): User
    getUsers: [User]
  }
```

165

```
`;

// Create PostgreSQL client
const client = new Client({
  user: 'your_username',
  host: 'localhost',
  database: 'your_database',
  password: 'your_password',
  port: 5432,
});

client.connect();

// Define resolvers to handle GraphQL queries
const resolvers = {
  Query: {
    getUser: async (_, { id }) => {
      const res = await client.query('SELECT * FROM users WHERE id = $1', [id]);
      return res.rows[0];
    },
    getUsers: async () => {
      const res = await client.query('SELECT * FROM users');
      return res.rows;
    },
  },
};

// Create Apollo Server instance
const server = new ApolloServer({ typeDefs, resolvers });

// Start the server
server.listen().then(({ url }) => {
  console.log(`Server ready at ${url}`);
});
```

4. Start the Server: Run the server using node:

bash

Copy

```
node server.js
```

This will start the GraphQL server on a specified port (usually 4000). You can now access the GraphQL playground at http://localhost:4000 and run queries such as:

graphql

Copy

```
query {
  getUsers {
    id
    name
    email
  }
}
```

The response will look like this:

json

Copy

```
{
  "data": {
    "getUsers": [
      {
        "id": "1",
        "name": "John Doe",
        "email": "john.doe@example.com"
      },
      {
        "id": "2",
        "name": "Jane Smith",
        "email": "jane.smith@example.com"
      }
    ]
  }
}
```

12.3.2 Optimizing GraphQL Queries for PostgreSQL

While integrating GraphQL with PostgreSQL allows flexibility, it's essential to optimize both the database queries and GraphQL schema for performance:

1. **Use Batching**: GraphQL queries often require fetching related data (e.g., fetching posts for a user). Rather than issuing multiple queries to PostgreSQL, use **DataLoader** or similar batching tools to batch database requests and reduce the number of database calls.

2. **Pagination**: When returning lists of data (e.g., a list of users), implement **pagination** to avoid loading too many records at once. GraphQL supports pagination through **cursor-based pagination** or **limit-offset pagination**.
Example of a paginated query:
graphql
Copy

```
query {
  getUsers(limit: 10, offset: 0) {
    id
    name
    email
  }
}
```

3. **Indexing**: Ensure that you are using **indexes** in PostgreSQL for frequently queried fields (e.g., id, email). Indexing improves the speed of read operations, especially when filtering or sorting large datasets.

12.4 Hybrid Architectures: Combining DynamoDB and PostgreSQL

In some applications, a **hybrid architecture** combining both **DynamoDB** and **PostgreSQL** can provide the best of both worlds. While **DynamoDB** offers speed and scalability for high-velocity, schema-less data, **PostgreSQL** provides relational data management with complex queries, joins, and transactional support.

A hybrid architecture allows you to take advantage of the strengths of both databases. For example, you might use DynamoDB to store high-velocity, semi-structured data such as logs, user sessions, and caching, while relying on PostgreSQL to handle relational data, such as transactions, user profiles, and other structured data.

12.4.1 Benefits of a Hybrid Architecture

1. **Performance Optimization**: By choosing the right database for the right task, you can optimize the performance of your application. DynamoDB excels in handling large-scale, low-latency operations, while PostgreSQL can handle complex queries and transactions.
2. **Cost Efficiency**: Each database offers different cost structures. For instance, DynamoDB's pricing model is based on throughput and storage, while PostgreSQL may be more cost-effective for complex queries in certain scenarios. A hybrid model lets you optimize cost based on usage.
3. **Data Flexibility**: DynamoDB offers schema-less flexibility for semi-structured data, while PostgreSQL provides robust relational structures for managing complex relationships and enforcing data integrity.

12.4.2 Implementing Hybrid Architectures

In a hybrid architecture, applications interact with both databases depending on the data access pattern. For example:

- **Use DynamoDB** for:
  - High-velocity, unstructured, or semi-structured data.
  - Real-time applications that require quick lookups and automatic scaling.
  - Session management, caching, and event-driven architectures.
- **Use PostgreSQL** for:
  - Complex queries, joins, and reporting.
  - Relational data where consistency and ACID (Atomicity, Consistency, Isolation, Durability) properties are crucial.
  - Transactional workflows and business logic that require relational integrity.

In such architectures, **AWS Lambda** can be used to facilitate seamless communication between DynamoDB and PostgreSQL, allowing for automated data synchronization and efficient handling of different data types.

12.5 Use Cases for Hybrid Databases in API Design

Hybrid database architectures are becoming increasingly popular for certain use cases where a single database cannot fulfill all the requirements of modern applications. By combining DynamoDB and PostgreSQL, you can optimize performance, scalability, and flexibility while managing different types of data in the most efficient way.

12.5.1 Use Case 1: Real-Time Applications with Transactional Data

In applications like **e-commerce** platforms, there may be a need for real-time updates of inventory (handled by DynamoDB) as well as transactional records like user orders (handled by PostgreSQL). Here's how the hybrid model works:

- **DynamoDB** handles real-time inventory updates and sessions where speed and scalability are crucial.
- **PostgreSQL** stores user orders, payments, and inventory adjustments, where data integrity, consistency, and relational queries are required.

This hybrid model ensures that the system can scale rapidly while maintaining consistency and transaction integrity for important business data.

12.5.2 Use Case 2: Logging and Analytics

In use cases such as **IoT (Internet of Things)** platforms or **analytics pipelines**, large amounts of raw data need to be ingested, processed, and analyzed. A hybrid approach can be used to handle both real-time data processing and analytics:

- **DynamoDB** stores large volumes of sensor data or event logs that are constantly generated in real time.
- **PostgreSQL** can then be used to store aggregated results, complex queries, and analysis reports.

This architecture allows real-time data ingestion and fast querying of analytics without overloading the relational database.

12.5.3 Use Case 3: Content Management Systems (CMS)

In a **CMS**, you might store user-generated content and multimedia files (such as images and videos) in **DynamoDB** due to its ability to handle large amounts of semi-structured data with high throughput. On the other hand, structured data such as user profiles, comments, and metadata can be stored in **PostgreSQL** for relational integrity and complex querying.

By using DynamoDB for high-volume data and PostgreSQL for relational data, you can efficiently manage content while providing flexible querying capabilities for both types of data.

Chapter 13: Future-Proofing Your API

13.1 Preparing for API Growth: Scalability Considerations

As your application grows and attracts more users, the API becomes a critical piece of the infrastructure. It's essential to plan for **scalability** from the outset to ensure that your API can handle increased traffic, data load, and evolving requirements. Scalability ensures that your API can grow seamlessly without compromising performance or availability. In this section, we'll explore scalability considerations that are vital for future-proofing your API.

13.1.1 Horizontal vs. Vertical Scalability

When it comes to scaling an API, you typically have two choices: **horizontal scaling** and **vertical scaling**. Both approaches come with their advantages and considerations.

- **Vertical Scaling** (Scaling Up): Vertical scaling involves adding more resources (CPU, memory, storage) to a single server or instance to handle more load. For example, upgrading an EC2 instance to a larger size in AWS or increasing the database's instance size in a managed cloud database service like Amazon RDS.
  Pros:
  - Simple to implement for small applications or short-term growth.
  - Suitable for non-distributed architectures.
- **Cons**:
  - Has physical limits on how much you can scale.
  - More prone to downtimes during upgrades.
  - Can lead to higher costs as resources become underutilized.
- **Horizontal Scaling** (Scaling Out): Horizontal scaling involves adding more instances of servers, services, or databases to distribute the load. With horizontal scaling, your system grows by adding more machines (servers or containers) to a pool, and each machine can handle a portion of the requests.
  Pros:
  - More flexible and capable of handling huge traffic increases.
  - Better fault tolerance; if one server goes down, others can take over.
  - Can be automated with cloud orchestration tools (e.g., AWS Auto Scaling, Kubernetes).

- **Cons**:
  - ○ Requires more complex infrastructure (load balancing, database sharding).
  - ○ Potentially higher operational costs due to more instances.
  - ○ Adds complexity to managing distributed systems (e.g., data consistency, network latency).

For APIs that need to handle rapid growth and varying loads, **horizontal scaling** is often the more sustainable approach. It's especially valuable when building microservices architectures, where individual components (e.g., authentication, user management) can scale independently.

13.1.2 Load Balancing

Load balancing plays a crucial role in scaling your API by distributing incoming requests across multiple servers, ensuring no single server becomes a bottleneck. There are two types of load balancing commonly used:

1. **Round Robin Load Balancing**: Requests are distributed evenly across servers in a circular pattern. This is the simplest form of load balancing and works well when all servers have the same capacity.
2. **Weighted Load Balancing**: Requests are distributed based on the server's performance capabilities. For instance, a server with higher resources (CPU, RAM) may receive a higher proportion of traffic.

Using **AWS Elastic Load Balancer (ELB)** or **NGINX** for load balancing can help ensure that requests are efficiently routed to available instances.

13.1.3 Caching to Reduce Load

To maintain performance as your API grows, it's important to reduce the load on your backend systems. **Caching** is an effective technique for improving response times and reducing database queries.

- **In-memory Caching**: Systems like **Redis** and **Memcached** provide fast, in-memory caching that stores the most frequently accessed data (e.g., API responses, user sessions) in RAM, drastically reducing response time for repeat requests.
  Use cases:
  - ○ Storing frequently queried data, such as user profiles or product catalogs.

- Caching database query results, especially for resource-intensive operations.
- Reducing load on backend systems and speeding up API response times.
- **Edge Caching**: **CDNs (Content Delivery Networks)** like **Amazon CloudFront** cache static resources closer to the user's location, reducing latency and improving load times for global users.
  Use cases:
  - Caching static content such as images, videos, and style sheets.
  - Reducing load on origin servers for high-traffic, globally distributed applications.

13.1.4 Database Scaling

As your API grows, your database can quickly become a bottleneck. Scaling your database to handle increased load requires planning.

- **Sharding**: Sharding involves partitioning your data across multiple database instances (shards). This is particularly useful for large-scale applications where data can be logically split into independent segments.
- **Read Replicas**: Use **read replicas** to distribute read queries across multiple database instances. This offloads read-heavy operations from the primary database, improving overall performance.
- **Database Indexing**: Ensure that your database is properly indexed, especially on frequently queried fields, to speed up search and retrieval times.

13.1.5 Auto-Scaling and Elasticity

In cloud environments, **auto-scaling** enables your infrastructure to automatically adjust based on real-time demand. Services like **AWS Auto Scaling** can increase or decrease the number of EC2 instances based on metrics like CPU usage, memory, and request rates.

For databases, services like **Amazon RDS** provide automatic scaling options for read replicas and storage, ensuring that your database can grow seamlessly to handle increasing traffic and data volume.

13.2 Serverless API Design: Benefits and Pitfalls

Serverless architecture is a cloud-native approach to building and running applications without the need to manage infrastructure. In the context of RESTful API design, **serverless APIs** use services like **AWS Lambda, API Gateway**, and **DynamoDB** to handle API requests and scale automatically based on traffic.

While serverless design offers several benefits, it also comes with unique challenges that need to be considered. In this section, we'll explore the benefits and pitfalls of serverless API design.

13.2.1 Benefits of Serverless API Design

1. **Automatic Scalability**: One of the most significant advantages of serverless architecture is that it automatically scales in response to incoming traffic. Services like **AWS Lambda** can scale from a few requests per second to thousands, depending on demand, without any manual intervention.
2. **Cost Efficiency**: Serverless platforms use a **pay-as-you-go** model, meaning you only pay for the compute time you use. There are no costs associated with idle servers, making serverless a highly cost-effective solution for APIs with unpredictable or low traffic.
3. **Reduced Operational Overhead**: With serverless, you don't have to manage servers, patching, or scaling. This significantly reduces operational complexity and allows developers to focus on writing application code rather than infrastructure management.
4. **Event-Driven Architecture**: Serverless APIs are often event-driven, where services like AWS Lambda respond to events (e.g., HTTP requests, database changes, file uploads) and perform specific actions. This can simplify the architecture, as you can focus on handling events rather than managing a sequence of steps in a traditional monolithic API.
5. **Faster Time-to-Market**: With the abstraction of server management, developers can quickly deploy and iterate on serverless APIs. This leads to faster time-to-market for new features and APIs, enabling organizations to stay competitive.
6. **Built-in Fault Tolerance**: Most serverless platforms offer built-in fault tolerance. For instance, AWS Lambda automatically retries failed executions, ensuring that your API is more resilient and less prone to downtime.

13.2.2 Pitfalls of Serverless API Design

While serverless design offers substantial benefits, there are certain challenges and considerations to keep in mind:

1. **Cold Starts**: One of the most common pitfalls of serverless architecture is the **cold start** problem. When a Lambda function is invoked for the first time (or after a period of inactivity), it may experience latency due to the initialization time required to spin up resources. This can result in delayed responses for some requests, particularly for high-performance applications where low latency is crucial.
   Mitigation: Cold starts can be mitigated by keeping functions warm with scheduled invocations, though this may add additional costs.

2. **State Management**: Serverless functions are stateless by design, which can make it difficult to manage session data or persistent state between invocations. For stateful applications, integrating **Amazon DynamoDB** or **Amazon S3** for external state storage is necessary.
   Mitigation: Use external storage options for managing session data, or consider serverless databases like DynamoDB, which provide high scalability and performance.

3. **Vendor Lock-In**: Serverless architectures often involve using specific cloud providers (e.g., AWS Lambda, Google Cloud Functions), which can result in **vendor lock-in**. This can make it difficult to migrate to other cloud providers or hybrid solutions in the future.
   Mitigation: While serverless applications can result in vendor lock-in, using open-source serverless frameworks (e.g., the **Serverless Framework**) can help mitigate this issue by abstracting cloud-specific APIs.

4. **Debugging and Monitoring**: Since serverless functions are ephemeral and run in a managed environment, debugging and monitoring can be challenging. Tracking down performance bottlenecks or understanding function invocations across distributed systems can require more sophisticated monitoring tools.
   Mitigation: Use cloud-native monitoring tools like **AWS CloudWatch** or third-party observability platforms (e.g., **Datadog**, **New Relic**) to capture logs, monitor performance, and trace function executions.

5. **Limited Execution Time**: Most serverless platforms, including AWS Lambda, have a maximum execution time limit for functions (e.g., 15 minutes for AWS Lambda). Long-running processes may need to be refactored into smaller, more manageable tasks.

Mitigation: Break down long-running tasks into smaller chunks and use services like **AWS Step Functions** to manage complex workflows with multiple steps.

13.3 Microservices and API Gateways for Large-Scale APIs

As your application grows in complexity, transitioning to a **microservices architecture** can be a highly effective strategy for managing large-scale APIs. Microservices allow you to break down your application into smaller, independently deployable services that each handle a specific business function. Paired with an **API Gateway**, this approach offers scalability, flexibility, and maintainability for modern APIs.

13.3.1 What are Microservices?

Microservices are a way of designing and developing software where the application is divided into small, independent services. Each microservice is responsible for a specific business functionality, such as user authentication, payment processing, or order management.

Microservices interact with each other through well-defined **APIs**, usually over HTTP/HTTPS or messaging queues. Each service has its own database and can be deployed, updated, or scaled independently, which helps in achieving agility and flexibility. Here's why microservices work so well for large-scale APIs:

- **Modularity**: Each microservice can be developed, deployed, and scaled independently, which allows different teams to work on different parts of the application without stepping on each other's toes.
- **Fault Isolation**: If one microservice fails, it doesn't affect the entire application, making it easier to isolate and address issues.
- **Scalability**: Microservices enable scaling at the service level. For instance, if the order service experiences a heavy load, it can be scaled independently without affecting other services, such as payment processing.
- **Flexibility**: Different services can be built with different programming languages, frameworks, and databases. This allows you to choose the best technology stack for each service.

13.3.2 Benefits of Using API Gateways

An **API Gateway** is an essential component of a microservices-based architecture. It acts as a single entry point for client requests, which are then routed to the appropriate
177

microservices. Here are the key benefits of using an API Gateway in a microservices architecture:

- **Centralized Management**: The API Gateway handles cross-cutting concerns such as authentication, rate limiting, logging, and caching, centralizing these functions in one place.
- **Request Routing**: The API Gateway routes incoming requests to the correct microservice. It abstracts the complexities of the internal architecture from clients, making the system simpler to interact with.
- **Security**: The API Gateway is the first line of defense against security threats. It can enforce authentication and authorization before forwarding requests to backend services.
- **Load Balancing**: It can distribute traffic across multiple instances of a microservice, improving availability and performance.
- **API Aggregation**: In a microservices architecture, multiple microservices might be needed to fulfill a single request. The API Gateway can aggregate responses from multiple services and return a unified response to the client, optimizing client interactions.

For instance, in a **shopping application**, the API Gateway might handle requests such as:

- Authenticating the user and passing the token to each service.
- Routing the user to the **user service** for profile data.
- Fetching product information from the **product service**.
- Retrieving shipping information from the **shipping service**.

By centralizing these interactions through the API Gateway, you significantly reduce complexity and improve the scalability of the system.

13.3.3 Considerations for Microservices and API Gateways

While microservices and API Gateways provide powerful benefits, there are challenges that come with this approach:

- **Service Coordination**: Managing the interactions between services can become complex, especially when there are many microservices. Service orchestration tools like **Kubernetes** or **AWS ECS** can help automate the management and deployment of services.

- **Data Consistency**: In a microservices architecture, each service has its own database. Managing data consistency across services, especially in eventual consistency models, requires careful design, such as using **saga patterns** or **CQRS** (Command Query Responsibility Segregation).
- **Complexity**: While microservices simplify the individual components, they can introduce complexities in terms of service discovery, API versioning, and network latency. Using a solid API Gateway and infrastructure management solution helps mitigate these issues.

13.4 Emerging Trends in Database Technologies

As the world of data continues to evolve, new trends and technologies are emerging to meet the needs of modern applications. These trends provide innovative ways to handle larger data volumes, scale applications faster, and offer better performance and flexibility. Here are some of the key emerging trends in database technologies.

13.4.1 Multi-Model Databases

A **multi-model database** supports more than one data model (e.g., document, key-value, graph) within the same database engine. This flexibility allows organizations to use the best model for each use case while avoiding the need to manage multiple types of databases. For example, **ArangoDB** and **Couchbase** provide multi-model databases that can store both relational and non-relational data.

Benefits:

- Reduces complexity by allowing multiple data models to coexist in a single database.
- Improves performance by choosing the right data model for specific use cases.
- Minimizes operational overhead by using a single database engine instead of multiple disparate systems.

13.4.2 Distributed SQL Databases

Distributed SQL databases, such as **CockroachDB** and **Google Spanner**, are designed to scale horizontally, much like NoSQL databases, while providing the familiar SQL interface and ACID-compliant transactions. These databases combine the benefits of relational databases (e.g., strong consistency, SQL queries) with the scalability features typically seen in NoSQL databases.

179

Benefits:

- **Horizontal scalability**: Distribute data across many nodes without sacrificing consistency or performance.
- **Global distribution**: Ideal for applications that require low-latency access across different regions.
- **SQL compatibility**: Retain the ability to use standard SQL queries while benefiting from scalability.

13.4.3 Blockchain Databases

Blockchain technology, originally designed for cryptocurrencies like Bitcoin, is now being explored for general-purpose database use. **Blockchain databases** offer features like immutable records, decentralized trust, and transparency. They are especially useful for applications that require audit trails, such as **financial systems**, **supply chain management**, and **healthcare**.

Benefits:

- **Immutability**: Once data is recorded, it cannot be changed, making it ideal for applications requiring audit trails or transparent data.
- **Decentralization**: Data is distributed across a network of nodes, reducing the risk of single points of failure and central control.
- **Trust**: The decentralized nature of blockchain provides built-in security and eliminates the need for intermediaries.

13.4.4 Serverless Databases

Serverless databases are fully managed databases that automatically scale based on usage, providing developers with a simple, cost-effective way to handle database operations without managing infrastructure. Examples include **Amazon Aurora Serverless** and **Azure Cosmos DB**.

Benefits:

- **Automatic scaling**: Database resources are dynamically allocated based on demand, ensuring optimal performance without manual intervention.
- **Pay-per-use**: You only pay for the database usage (compute and storage), making serverless databases cost-efficient for workloads with variable traffic patterns.

- **Simplified management**: Serverless databases automatically handle backups, patching, and scaling, reducing operational complexity.

13.5 Preparing for the Future of API Development with NoSQL and SQL

As the landscape of database technologies continues to evolve, it's essential to prepare your API for future demands by understanding both **NoSQL** and **SQL** databases. Both types of databases offer distinct advantages and limitations, and understanding when to use each can help you design APIs that are efficient, flexible, and future-proof.

13.5.1 The Rise of NoSQL Databases

NoSQL databases like **MongoDB**, **Cassandra**, and **DynamoDB** are growing in popularity due to their ability to handle large volumes of unstructured or semi-structured data with high scalability and flexibility. They are ideal for use cases such as real-time applications, big data, IoT, and applications with rapidly changing schema requirements.

- **Flexible Data Models**: NoSQL databases don't require a predefined schema, making it easier to evolve the structure as the application grows.
- **Scalability**: NoSQL databases excel at scaling horizontally, making them suitable for high-volume applications.
- **Performance**: Optimized for high read and write throughput, often at the expense of strict data consistency.

As businesses continue to handle more unstructured data, NoSQL databases will likely play an increasing role in API development. However, for applications that require **ACID compliance**, **complex queries**, or **strong relationships** between data entities, SQL databases will still be necessary.

13.5.2 The Continued Relevance of SQL Databases

SQL databases like **PostgreSQL**, **MySQL**, and **Microsoft SQL Server** continue to be the backbone of many enterprise applications, especially those that require complex relationships, transactional consistency, and extensive reporting capabilities.

- **Relational Data Models**: SQL databases excel in managing structured data with relationships, making them ideal for applications that require joins, foreign keys, and complex queries.

- **ACID Compliance**: SQL databases are designed to ensure data integrity and consistency with **ACID transactions**, which is crucial for applications like financial systems, e-commerce platforms, and enterprise applications.
- **Mature Ecosystem**: SQL databases have been around for decades, making them well-understood and supported by a large ecosystem of tools and resources.

Despite the rise of NoSQL, SQL databases remain critical in applications that require structured data storage, complex querying, and relational consistency. However, as more businesses adopt hybrid models and microservices architectures, SQL and NoSQL databases will increasingly coexist in the same application.

13.5.3 Hybrid Data Architectures

As businesses increasingly operate in multi-cloud and hybrid environments, combining SQL and NoSQL databases in a single API is becoming more common. By using **hybrid data architectures**, businesses can leverage the benefits of both SQL and NoSQL systems.

For example:

- **NoSQL** might be used for fast, real-time data storage such as session management, caching, or user logs.
- **SQL** could be used for structured data requiring transactional consistency, such as financial transactions, user profiles, and product catalogs.

Hybrid architectures can leverage the strengths of both data models, ensuring that the right technology is used for each type of data, and enhancing API performance, flexibility, and scalability.

Chapter 14: Real-World Case Studies

14.1 Case Study 1: Building an E-Commerce API with DynamoDB

E-commerce platforms require high-performance, low-latency APIs to manage large volumes of user interactions, product listings, and transactional data. DynamoDB, with its scalable, low-latency performance and fully managed nature, is an ideal choice for powering e-commerce APIs. In this case study, we'll explore how DynamoDB can be used to build an e-commerce API capable of handling large volumes of products, orders, and customer interactions.

14.1.1 Business Requirements

The business goal is to build a fast, scalable API to support an e-commerce platform that can handle a high volume of customers, product inventory, and transactions. The API should:

- Support high-frequency reads and writes as customers browse products and place orders.
- Be highly available and scalable to handle traffic spikes during sales or peak shopping seasons.
- Ensure low-latency responses for product lookups and user data retrieval.
- Allow easy management and querying of product categories, prices, inventory, and customer orders.

14.1.2 System Design

To meet the requirements of the e-commerce platform, DynamoDB is used to store the primary entities of the system: **users**, **products**, and **orders**. DynamoDB's fast, highly scalable performance and its ability to handle unstructured data made it an optimal choice. We'll use a **single-table design**, which is common in DynamoDB to optimize for read and write efficiency, while keeping the database flexible and fast.

Tables and Key Design

1. **Users Table**:
    - **Partition Key**: userID (string)
    - **Sort Key**: orderID (string, for storing order history)
    - **Attributes**: Name, email, shipping address, payment methods, etc.

    This table stores user profiles, including their information and their order history.

2. **Products Table**:
   - **Partition Key**: categoryID (string)
   - **Sort Key**: productID (string)
   - **Attributes**: Product name, description, price, stock count, reviews, etc.

   This table stores product data. Products are grouped by category for efficient querying (e.g., browsing all electronics).
3. **Orders Table**:
   - **Partition Key**: userID (string)
   - **Sort Key**: orderID (string)
   - **Attributes**: Order date, order total, product IDs, shipping status, etc.

   This table stores customer orders. The userID partition key allows quick retrieval of all orders made by a user.

Data Access Patterns and Indexing

DynamoDB requires careful planning of **access patterns**. In this e-commerce system, we need to:

- Retrieve products by category.
- Retrieve product details by product ID.
- Track order history for each user.
- Query a user's specific orders based on timestamps.

We'll also use **Global Secondary Indexes (GSIs)** to optimize read operations for specific access patterns:

- **GSI for Product Price**: This allows the system to query products by their price range, useful for features like price filtering in the product catalog.
- **GSI for Product Reviews**: This index will enable the API to efficiently fetch products based on average user ratings.

14.1.3 API Design

The e-commerce API is designed to handle common interactions, including product browsing, user account management, and order processing. Here are the key endpoints:

1. **GET /products**:
   - Fetch products by category, price range, and/or rating.
   - Leverage DynamoDB queries and the product category index to quickly retrieve products.

Example query:
graphql
Copy
```
query {
  products(categoryID: "electronics", priceRange: {min: 100, max: 500}, rating: 4) {
    id
    name
    description
    price
  }
}
```

2. **GET /users/{userID}/orders**:
   - Fetch a user's orders by order ID or date.
   - Use the userID and orderID sort key to retrieve order history.

Example query:
graphql
Copy
```
query {
  userOrders(userID: "1234") {
    orderID
    total
    products {
      name
      price
    }
  }
}
```

3. **POST /orders**:
   - Create a new order when a user checks out.
   - The order data (product IDs, quantities, user shipping address) is stored in the **Orders** table.

Example request:
json
Copy

```
{
 "userID": "1234",
 "orderID": "5678",
 "products": [
   {"productID": "abcd", "quantity": 2},
   {"productID": "efgh", "quantity": 1}
 ],
 "total": 299.99,
 "shippingStatus": "Processing"
}
```

4. **POST /users/{userID}/reviews**:
   - Submit a review for a product.
   - Store the review data in the **Products** table and update the average product rating.

Example request:
json
Copy

```
{
 "userID": "1234",
 "productID": "abcd",
 "rating": 4,
 "comment": "Great product!"
}
```

14.1.4 Scaling and Performance Optimization

As the e-commerce platform grows, ensuring the system can handle traffic spikes during sales events (e.g., Black Friday) is crucial. Here's how the system is designed to scale:

1. **Provisioned Capacity vs. On-Demand Mode**: DynamoDB offers two capacity modes: **Provisioned** and **On-Demand**. For predictable workloads, provisioned capacity can be set for **Read Capacity Units (RCUs)** and **Write Capacity Units**

(WCUs), while for variable traffic, **On-Demand** mode is beneficial because it automatically scales based on request volume.

2. **Auto Scaling**: DynamoDB's **auto-scaling** capabilities help manage fluctuating traffic. DynamoDB automatically adjusts throughput capacity to meet the demand without requiring manual intervention.

3. **Caching with Amazon ElastiCache**: To reduce read pressure on DynamoDB, frequently accessed data (e.g., product details, popular categories) is cached in **ElastiCache (Redis)**. This allows for faster retrieval and reduces DynamoDB costs by lowering the number of queries.

4. **Read Replicas**: Use **DynamoDB Global Tables** or **DynamoDB Accelerator (DAX)** to distribute read traffic across multiple regions, ensuring low-latency access for customers worldwide.

14.2 Case Study 2: Building a Social Media API with PostgreSQL

Building a **social media API** comes with its own set of requirements: handling user profiles, posts, comments, likes, and relationships (e.g., following, friends). While DynamoDB works well for unstructured data and fast reads, **PostgreSQL** is the preferred choice for relational data and complex queries, such as handling user relationships, performing joins, and ensuring data consistency.

In this case study, we'll discuss how to build a social media API using PostgreSQL as the backend database.

14.2.1 Business Requirements

The social media platform needs an API that can:

- Manage user profiles, posts, comments, and interactions (likes, shares).
- Allow users to follow others, comment on posts, and like content.
- Ensure data consistency and support complex queries for retrieving user posts, timelines, and comments.
- Provide the ability to scale the API as user activity grows.

14.2.2 System Design

PostgreSQL is chosen for its **ACID compliance, support for complex joins**, and **advanced querying capabilities**. We'll use **PostgreSQL's relational model** to store and manage structured data, including users, posts, and comments.

187

Tables and Key Design

1. **Users Table:**
   - **Columns**: user_id, name, email, password, created_at
   - The user_id is the primary key, uniquely identifying each user.
2. **Posts Table:**
   - **Columns**: post_id, user_id (foreign key to Users), content, created_at
   - The user_id establishes the relationship between posts and the users who created them.
3. **Comments Table:**
   - **Columns**: comment_id, post_id (foreign key to Posts), user_id (foreign key to Users), content, created_at
   - This table tracks comments on individual posts, allowing users to interact with content.
4. **Likes Table:**
   - **Columns**: like_id, post_id (foreign key to Posts), user_id (foreign key to Users), created_at
   - This table records likes for posts, establishing a relationship between users and the posts they like.
5. **Follows Table:**
   - **Columns**: follow_id, follower_id (foreign key to Users), followee_id (foreign key to Users), created_at
   - This table tracks user relationships, allowing users to follow each other.

Data Access Patterns

The key queries in a social media API involve retrieving posts, user timelines, and managing interactions like comments, likes, and follows.

1. **GET /users/{user_id}/posts:**
   - Retrieve all posts for a given user.

Example query:
graphql
Copy

```
query {
 userPosts(userID: "1234") {
  content
  created_at
 }
```

}

2. **GET /users/{user_id}/timeline**:
    - Fetch the posts of users that the current user follows. This requires joining the **Follows** table with the **Posts** table.

Example query:
graphql
Copy

```
query {
  userTimeline(userID: "1234") {
    postID
    content
    created_at
  }
}
```

3. **POST /posts**:
    - Create a new post for the authenticated user.

Example request:
json
Copy

```
{
  "user_id": "1234",
  "content": "Just joined this amazing platform!",
  "created_at": "2025-02-12T10:00:00"
}
```

4. **POST /comments**:
    - Post a comment on a specific post.

Example request:
json
Copy

```
{
  "post_id": "5678",
```

189

```
"user_id": "1234",
"content": "Great post!",
"created_at": "2025-02-12T11:00:00"
}
```

5. **POST /likes**:
   - Like a specific post.

Example request:
json
Copy
```
{
 "post_id": "5678",
 "user_id": "1234",
 "created_at": "2025-02-12T11:05:00"
}
```

14.2.3 API Design

The API should support common social media actions like user registration, posting content, commenting, liking, and following users. The **RESTful API** design uses HTTP methods like GET, POST, PUT, and DELETE to interact with the database.

Endpoints:

- **GET /users/{user_id}/posts**: Fetch all posts by a user.
- **GET /users/{user_id}/timeline**: Get the posts from the users the current user follows.
- **POST /posts**: Create a new post.
- **POST /comments**: Create a comment on a post.
- **POST /likes**: Like a post.
- **POST /follows**: Follow another user.

14.2.4 Scaling and Performance Optimization

- **Indexing**: PostgreSQL indexes the user_id and post_id fields in the **Posts, Comments**, and **Likes** tables to speed up queries.

- **Caching**: Use **Redis** to cache user timelines and posts to reduce the load on PostgreSQL during high-traffic periods.
- **Pagination**: Implement pagination for timeline queries to reduce the amount of data returned at once.

14.3 Case Study 3: Hybrid Database Solution for a Fintech API

In the **fintech** industry, managing financial transactions, user profiles, and regulatory compliance requires both **high scalability** and **strict data consistency**. **Hybrid database solutions**, which combine the strengths of both **SQL** and **NoSQL** databases, are becoming increasingly popular in this space to ensure optimal performance and reliability. This case study explores how a **fintech company** designed an API using both **PostgreSQL** for transactional consistency and **DynamoDB** for scalability and low-latency operations.

14.3.1 Business Requirements

The fintech company wanted to build a secure, reliable, and scalable API to manage the following core functionalities:

- **User Profiles**: Storing and managing customer data securely.
- **Transactions**: Handling financial transactions with a high degree of accuracy and consistency.
- **Analytics**: Providing insights into transaction history, account balances, and other financial metrics in near real-time.
- **Compliance**: Ensuring the solution adheres to financial regulations and can track transaction history for auditing purposes.

The solution needed to:

- Provide **high scalability** to handle unpredictable spikes in transaction volume, especially during peak hours.
- Ensure **ACID compliance** for transactional operations to prevent inconsistencies in financial data.
- Maintain **real-time transaction processing** while supporting analytical workloads on historical transaction data.
- Enable **easy data retrieval** for analytics and reporting, which required handling complex queries, aggregations, and joins.

191

14.3.2 System Design: Hybrid Approach

To meet these requirements, the company decided to implement a **hybrid database architecture** using **PostgreSQL** and **DynamoDB**.

1. **PostgreSQL for Transactional Data**: PostgreSQL was used for storing transactional data where consistency and relational integrity were critical. Financial transactions are inherently relational, and operations like transfers, balances, and compliance checks require ACID (Atomicity, Consistency, Isolation, and Durability) properties to ensure correctness.
   The core tables in PostgreSQL include:
   - **Users Table**: Stores user details (user ID, personal information, and account status).
   - **Transactions Table**: Stores records of each financial transaction (user ID, amount, transaction type, timestamp, status).
   - **Account Balances Table**: Tracks the balance of each user's account, with a reference to the **Users** table.

Example schema for **Transactions**:
sql
Copy
```
CREATE TABLE transactions (
    transaction_id SERIAL PRIMARY KEY,
    user_id INTEGER REFERENCES users(user_id),
    amount DECIMAL(10, 2),
    transaction_type VARCHAR(50),
    status VARCHAR(50),
    created_at TIMESTAMP DEFAULT CURRENT_TIMESTAMP
);
```

2. **DynamoDB for High-Volume, Low-Latency Data**: **DynamoDB** was used to handle high-frequency data that needed to be accessed quickly but didn't necessarily require complex relational structures. The system needed to store large volumes of transaction logs, logs of user activities, and historical records for analytics.
   DynamoDB tables were designed to handle:
   - **Transaction Logs**: A log of all transactions for real-time processing.
   - **Activity Logs**: Logs of user activity, such as login attempts, account updates, and browsing activities.

- o **Analytical Data**: Real-time and aggregated transaction data for dashboards, reports, and analytics.

3. **DynamoDB Schema**:
   - o **Partition Key**: user_id
   - o **Sort Key**: timestamp (for logging user activities or transaction events by time)

Example schema for **Transaction Logs** in DynamoDB:
json
Copy

```
{
  "user_id": "1234",
  "timestamp": "2025-02-12T10:00:00Z",
  "transaction_id": "5678",
  "amount": "100.00",
  "transaction_type": "credit",
  "status": "completed"
}
```

14.3.3 API Design

The fintech API needed to interact with both **PostgreSQL** and **DynamoDB** to support a wide variety of operations, including transaction processing, user management, and real-time analytics. Key API endpoints include:

1. **POST /users**: Create a new user.
   - o Data is stored in **PostgreSQL** for user profile and identity management.
2. **POST /transactions**: Initiate a new transaction.
   - o The transaction is processed using **PostgreSQL**, ensuring ACID compliance.
   - o Real-time transaction data is recorded in **DynamoDB** for quick access and analysis.

Example request:
json
Copy

```
{
  "user_id": "1234",
```

```
"amount": "50.00",
"transaction_type": "withdrawal",
"status": "pending"
}
```

3. **GET /users/{user_id}/transactions**: Retrieve a user's transaction history.
   - **PostgreSQL** is used for detailed querying of past transactions, including joins with account balances, statuses, and timestamps.
   - **DynamoDB** is queried for real-time updates or high-frequency transactional logs.
4. **GET /analytics**: Fetch analytics and insights, such as total transaction volume, balance history, or financial reports.
   - Aggregated data from **DynamoDB** is used for near real-time analytics, enabling users to quickly access financial data without causing strain on the primary database.

14.3.4 Performance and Scalability

To ensure the system could handle millions of transactions per day and scale as the user base grows, several strategies were employed:

1. **Sharding and Partitioning**: In PostgreSQL, **partitioning** tables based on user ID or transaction date helps with large data volumes, while **horizontal scaling** of DynamoDB ensures that each database is capable of handling growing traffic.
2. **DynamoDB Global Tables**: By using **Global Tables**, transaction logs and activity data were replicated across multiple AWS regions, ensuring low-latency reads and improved fault tolerance for users worldwide.
3. **Auto-Scaling**: **DynamoDB Auto Scaling** was enabled to ensure that throughput capacity adjusts automatically based on incoming request volume, reducing the chances of throttling during peak transaction periods.
4. **Data Aggregation**: Aggregated transaction data is stored in DynamoDB, which allows for efficient querying of high-level metrics (e.g., total transaction volume by day, month, or year) without burdening PostgreSQL.
5. **Caching**: Frequently queried data, such as user profiles and balances, was cached in **Amazon ElastiCache** (Redis), reducing read load on both databases and improving API response times.

14.4 Lessons Learned and Takeaways

Building scalable and reliable APIs for complex systems such as e-commerce, social media, and fintech platforms presents unique challenges. By examining the case studies above, we can extract key insights and lessons learned that can be applied to other API design projects.

14.4.1 Key Takeaways from the E-Commerce API

1. **Careful Data Modeling is Critical**: The **single-table design** in DynamoDB is a powerful technique, but it requires careful thought regarding access patterns. Ensure that your table schema and indexes are designed to meet the most frequent queries of your application.
2. **Scalability is Not Just About Data Storage**: Caching frequently accessed data, like product details, helps to reduce load on the database and significantly improve response times for end-users. Integrating **Amazon ElastiCache** with DynamoDB proved to be a great way to manage read-heavy workloads.
3. **Choose the Right Database for the Right Use Case**: DynamoDB is excellent for handling high-throughput, low-latency requirements, but for complex querying and transactions, PostgreSQL is the better choice. For e-commerce platforms, **combining DynamoDB for catalog data** and **PostgreSQL for transactions** allowed us to balance performance and consistency.

14.4.2 Key Takeaways from the Social Media API

1. **PostgreSQL is Ideal for Relational Data**: PostgreSQL's ability to handle relational data and complex queries made it the right choice for storing social media interactions, where relationships between users and posts are crucial. Implementing **JOINs** and foreign key constraints helped maintain data integrity.
2. **Use Appropriate Caching for User-Facing Data**: By caching frequently accessed data, like user timelines, we significantly reduced the load on PostgreSQL. **Redis caching** was instrumental in ensuring fast access to user data during high traffic.
3. **Optimizing for Scalability**: Pagination and proper indexing are essential for managing large volumes of user-generated content. Efficiently indexing the post_id, user_id, and timestamp fields allowed the API to scale efficiently.

14.4.3 Key Takeaways from the Fintech API

1. **Hybrid Database Models Improve Flexibility**: A hybrid approach, using **PostgreSQL for transactional consistency** and **DynamoDB for high-performance analytics**, provides the flexibility needed for fintech applications. Each database was used for the right purpose, ensuring both high performance and regulatory compliance.
2. **Compliance is a Priority**: In fintech, compliance with financial regulations is critical. Data consistency, especially for transactions, should always be ensured. **PostgreSQL's ACID compliance** is vital for maintaining integrity in financial transactions.
3. **Scalability and Real-Time Data Are Key**: For large-scale applications like fintech, the ability to handle real-time transaction data and scale across multiple regions is essential. Using **DynamoDB's Global Tables** and **AWS Lambda** for real-time processing helped build a robust, scalable system.

Chapter 15: Bonus Resources

15.1 API Code Templates and Starter Projects

When developing APIs, having access to code templates and starter projects can significantly streamline the development process. These resources provide a strong foundation, saving you time in setting up essential features such as routing, authentication, database integration, and error handling. They help ensure that your API follows best practices, from structuring code to managing scalability. In this section, we'll explore useful **API code templates** and **starter projects** that can accelerate your API development.

15.1.1 Benefits of API Code Templates and Starter Projects

1. **Reduced Development Time**: Using code templates and starter projects gives you a ready-to-use structure for your API. This allows you to focus on business logic, reducing the time spent on repetitive tasks like setting up routing, database connections, or authentication.
2. **Best Practices from the Start**: These templates often follow industry best practices, which helps ensure your API is built using modern, efficient, and secure approaches. This includes proper handling of requests, error responses, and the separation of concerns in your application architecture.
3. **Modularity and Customization**: Templates can be easily customized and extended based on specific project requirements. For example, a template designed for a RESTful API can be modified to fit the needs of a GraphQL API by changing how data is fetched or adding resolvers.
4. **Easy Integration with Tools and Frameworks**: Starter projects typically integrate with popular frameworks and tools like **Node.js**, **Express**, **Flask**, **Django**, and **Spring Boot**, which simplifies the integration of other components such as databases, authentication, logging, and monitoring tools.

15.1.2 Popular API Code Templates

Here are some of the best API templates available for different programming languages and frameworks. These resources are ready to use and can be customized to meet the needs of any API project.

1. **Node.js / Express API Template**:
   - **Overview**: Express is one of the most popular frameworks for building APIs in Node.js. Starter projects typically include routing, middleware for error handling, user authentication (e.g., JWT), and a connection to a database (such as MongoDB or PostgreSQL).
   - **Features**:
     - User authentication with **JWT tokens**.
     - Input validation and sanitization.
     - Middleware for logging and error handling.
     - Modular routes for different resources (users, posts, etc.).
   - **Example Starter Projects**:
     - **express-api-starter**: A boilerplate project for quickly setting up a RESTful API with Express.
     - **node-rest-api-template**: A template with a fully functional authentication system using **passport.js**.
2. **GitHub Repositories**:
   - Express API Starter Project
   - Node.js API Starter
3. **Flask API Template (Python)**:
   - **Overview**: Flask is a lightweight Python framework that is commonly used for building APIs. Flask-based starter projects include basic routing, middleware, and optional integrations with databases like **PostgreSQL** or **MongoDB**.
   - **Features**:
     - Simple routing and request handling.
     - JWT-based authentication and session management.
     - Database integrations with **SQLAlchemy** or **MongoDB**.
     - Error handling and logging configurations.
   - **Example Starter Projects**:
     - **flask-api-starter**: A basic Flask application template with RESTful routes.
     - **flask-jwt-api**: A template to help build APIs with JWT authentication.
4. **GitHub Repositories**:
   - Flask REST API Starter
   - Flask JWT Auth
5. **Django REST Framework (Python)**:
   - **Overview**: Django, combined with Django REST Framework (DRF), offers a powerful setup for building scalable, production-ready APIs.

Starter projects for Django typically include user authentication, CRUD operations, and built-in admin interfaces for easier content management.

- ○ **Features**:
  - Admin interface for managing resources.
  - Robust user authentication and permissions with **Django REST Framework**.
  - Automatic documentation generation using **Swagger** or **OpenAPI**.
- ○ **Example Starter Projects**:
  - **django-rest-framework-starter**: A basic Django API project with JWT authentication.
  - **django-rest-framework-boilerplate**: A production-grade template for setting up APIs with JWT authentication, CORS, and user management.

6. **GitHub Repositories**:
   - ○ Django REST Framework Starter
   - ○ Django API Boilerplate

7. **Spring Boot API Template (Java)**:
   - ○ **Overview**: Spring Boot is a widely used Java framework for building production-grade APIs. It provides extensive functionality for building secure and scalable APIs, with features such as dependency injection, RESTful endpoints, and built-in security mechanisms.
   - ○ **Features**:
     - RESTful services with **Spring Web**.
     - Security using **Spring Security** (including OAuth and JWT).
     - Integration with **JPA** (Java Persistence API) for database interaction.
     - Built-in error handling and exception management.
   - ○ **Example Starter Projects**:
     - **spring-boot-api-starter**: A Spring Boot template that sets up essential features for building secure REST APIs.
     - **spring-boot-jwt-auth-api**: A starter template for Spring Boot APIs that includes JWT-based authentication and authorization.

8. **GitHub Repositories**:
   - ○ Spring Boot Starter
   - ○ Spring Boot JWT Authentication

15.1.3 How to Use These Starter Projects

1. **Clone the Repository**: Clone the repository of your chosen starter project to get the basic template.
   bash
   Copy
   git clone https://github.com/your-chosen-repository.git

2. **Install Dependencies**: Follow the instructions in the README.md file to install necessary dependencies. For example, using **npm** or **pip** for Python projects, or **maven** for Java projects.
   bash
   Copy
   npm install   # For Node.js projects
   pip install -r requirements.txt   # For Python/Flask/Django projects
   mvn install   # For Java/Spring Boot projects

3. **Set Up the Database**: For projects that require a database, configure the connection details in the project's configuration file. This may involve setting up environment variables or modifying config files for PostgreSQL, MySQL, or MongoDB.

4. **Run the Project**: After installing dependencies and setting up the database, run the server locally and test the API endpoints.
   bash
   Copy
   npm start   # For Node.js projects
   python app.py   # For Flask projects
   python manage.py runserver   # For Django projects
   mvn spring-boot:run   # For Spring Boot projects

5. **Start Developing**: With the template up and running, you can now begin customizing the API to meet your project's needs, adding new routes, integrating with third-party services, and implementing specific business logic.

15.2 GitHub Repositories with Working Examples

GitHub is an invaluable resource for developers looking for working examples of API projects, including templates, starter kits, and reference implementations. These repositories provide a wealth of pre-built solutions that can help you kick-start development or serve as a learning resource for understanding API best practices.

15.2.1 Why GitHub Repositories Are Invaluable

GitHub repositories contain:

- **Open-source code**: Access to a wide range of pre-written code that you can modify, customize, and build upon.
- **Collaboration**: Many repositories support collaborative development, where multiple developers contribute to a project, ensuring ongoing maintenance and feature expansion.
- **Community**: GitHub allows you to engage with the community, ask questions, submit issues, and contribute to the project.
- **Documentation**: Most repositories include detailed documentation, including instructions for setup, dependencies, and usage, making it easy to get started.

15.2.2 Popular GitHub Repositories for API Projects

1. **Awesome-API**:
   - **Overview**: This is a curated list of **open-source API-related projects** on GitHub, featuring API frameworks, tools, and examples. It's an excellent resource for discovering codebases, learning about different approaches to API design, and exploring technologies.
   - **Features**:
     - Categorized API projects (e.g., REST, GraphQL, WebSocket).
     - Examples for **multiple languages and frameworks** (e.g., Node.js, Python, Java, Go).
     - Links to tutorials, guides, and documentation.
   - **GitHub Link**: Awesome-API
2. **API Platform**:
   - **Overview**: API Platform is a **PHP framework** that simplifies the creation of RESTful APIs. This repository provides a full-featured framework for building modern web services.
   - **Features**:
     - A simple yet powerful framework for creating **REST APIs**.

- Support for **GraphQL** out of the box.
- Integrates easily with **Doctrine ORM** for database interaction.
- Includes features like pagination, filtering, and serialization.
  - **GitHub Link**: API Platform
3. **GraphQL API Boilerplate**:
   - **Overview**: A boilerplate project for building **GraphQL APIs** using **Node.js**. This repository includes a simple GraphQL server, a sample database connection (PostgreSQL), and basic query and mutation functionality.
   - **Features**:
     - Includes **Apollo Server** and **Express.js** for handling HTTP requests.
     - Demonstrates how to set up a **GraphQL schema**, resolvers, and database interactions.
     - Provides a basic authentication mechanism with JWT.
   - **GitHub Link**: GraphQL API Boilerplate
4. **FastAPI**:
   - **Overview**: FastAPI is a **Python framework** for building APIs quickly and with minimal code. It's known for being extremely fast (hence the name), with automatic generation of OpenAPI documentation.
   - **Features**:
     - **Fast performance** for building REST APIs.
     - Easy integration with **SQLAlchemy** for database management.
     - Automatic documentation generation using **Swagger** or **Redoc**.
   - **GitHub Link**: FastAPI
5. **Spring Boot API Example**:
   - **Overview**: This repository offers an example of **Spring Boot** used to create REST APIs. It's a great starting point for those looking to build APIs in Java with Spring.
   - **Features**:
     - Includes **Spring Security** for authentication and authorization.
     - **H2 database** integration for quick setup.
     - Example of using **Swagger UI** to document the API.
   - **GitHub Link**: Spring Boot API Example

15.2.3 How to Use GitHub Repositories for API Development

1. **Clone the Repository**: Start by cloning the repository to your local machine:
   bash
   Copy
   ```
   git clone https://github.com/username/repository.git
   ```

2. **Install Dependencies**: Follow the instructions in the repository's README.md file to install necessary dependencies.
   - For **Node.js** projects, run npm install.
   - For **Python** projects, run pip install -r requirements.txt.
3. **Configure the Database and Environment**: Many repositories require you to set up a database or environment variables. Make sure to adjust configuration files such as .env or config.js to suit your development environment.
4. **Run the Project Locally**: Once everything is set up, you can run the project using the commands provided in the documentation:
   bash
   Copy
   ```
   npm start       # For Node.js projects
   python app.py   # For Python projects
   mvn spring-boot:run   # For Spring Boot projects
   ```

5. **Explore and Customize**: Explore the example API endpoints and start customizing the code to fit your needs, such as adding new features, integrating third-party services, or changing database configurations.

15.3 Cloud Infrastructure Templates for AWS

Building and deploying APIs often requires robust cloud infrastructure to ensure reliability, scalability, and security. With **AWS** (Amazon Web Services), developers can leverage a wide array of cloud services to build, deploy, and scale their APIs efficiently. Cloud infrastructure templates for AWS can significantly speed up the process of setting up the environment and deploying your application while following best practices for scalability and cost management.

15.3.1 What Are Cloud Infrastructure Templates?

Cloud infrastructure templates are pre-defined configurations that allow you to set up and manage cloud resources without manually configuring each component. AWS provides tools such as **AWS CloudFormation** and **AWS CDK (Cloud Development Kit)**, which enable developers to define infrastructure resources in a declarative manner.

By using infrastructure templates, you can automate the process of creating and managing cloud resources, ensuring that your infrastructure is consistent, reproducible, and versioned.

15.3.2 AWS CloudFormation Templates for API Deployment

AWS CloudFormation allows you to define your entire infrastructure as code using a **JSON** or **YAML** template. These templates specify the resources needed to support your application, such as compute instances (e.g., **EC2**), databases (e.g., **RDS**), networking components (e.g., **VPC, subnets**), and security settings (e.g., **IAM roles**).

Here's an example of a **CloudFormation template** to set up an environment for an API backend:

```yaml
Copy
AWSTemplateFormatVersion: '2010-09-09'
Resources:
  ApiGateway:
    Type: 'AWS::ApiGateway::RestApi'
    Properties:
      Name: 'MyApi'
      Description: 'API for handling requests'

  LambdaExecutionRole:
    Type: 'AWS::IAM::Role'
    Properties:
      AssumeRolePolicyDocument:
        Version: '2012-10-17'
        Statement:
          - Action: 'sts:AssumeRole'
            Effect: 'Allow'
            Principal:
```

```yaml
        Service: 'lambda.amazonaws.com'
  Policies:
   - PolicyName: 'LambdaExecutionPolicy'
     PolicyDocument:
      Version: '2012-10-17'
      Statement:
       - Action: 'logs:*'
         Effect: 'Allow'
         Resource: '*'

LambdaFunction:
  Type: 'AWS::Lambda::Function'
  Properties:
   Handler: 'index.handler'
   Role: !GetAtt LambdaExecutionRole.Arn
   FunctionName: 'MyApiFunction'
   Runtime: 'nodejs14.x'
   Code:
    S3Bucket: 'myBucket'
    S3Key: 'lambda-code.zip'

ApiGatewayMethod:
  Type: 'AWS::ApiGateway::Method'
  Properties:
   AuthorizationType: NONE
   HttpMethod: GET
   ResourceId: !GetAtt ApiGateway.RootResourceId
   RestApiId: !Ref ApiGateway
   Integration:
    IntegrationHttpMethod: POST
    Type: AWS_PROXY
    Uri: !Sub
'arn:aws:apigateway:${AWS::Region}:lambda:path/2015-03-31/functions/${LambdaFu
nction.Arn}/invocations'

Outputs:
 ApiUrl:
  Value: !Sub
'https://${ApiGateway}.execute-api.${AWS::Region}.amazonaws.com/prod'
```

205

Description: 'API URL'

This template creates the following resources:

- An **API Gateway** REST API.
- An **AWS Lambda function** to handle requests.
- An **IAM role** for the Lambda function to access CloudWatch logs.
- A method in the API Gateway to trigger the Lambda function using AWS Proxy integration.

15.3.3 Benefits of Using AWS CloudFormation Templates

1. **Automation**: With CloudFormation, you can automate the entire deployment process, making it easy to replicate environments across different stages (development, staging, production).
2. **Consistency**: CloudFormation ensures that every deployment is consistent with the defined template, avoiding manual configuration errors.
3. **Cost Management**: By defining resources as code, you can track and optimize your cloud usage. CloudFormation makes it easy to modify, delete, or scale infrastructure components as your requirements evolve.
4. **Version Control**: CloudFormation templates can be stored in version control systems (like **Git**), allowing teams to track changes to infrastructure and roll back to previous versions if necessary.

15.3.4 AWS CDK for Infrastructure as Code

The **AWS Cloud Development Kit (CDK)** is another powerful tool for managing infrastructure as code. Unlike CloudFormation, which uses JSON or YAML templates, the **AWS CDK** allows you to define infrastructure using familiar programming languages like **TypeScript**, **Python**, **Java**, and **C#**.

The AWS CDK simplifies defining cloud resources, enables the use of imperative logic, and offers a more flexible approach to managing infrastructure.

Example using **AWS CDK in TypeScript** to deploy a Lambda function and API Gateway:

```typescript
Copy
import * as cdk from 'aws-cdk-lib';
```

```
import * as lambda from 'aws-cdk-lib/aws-lambda';
import * as apigateway from 'aws-cdk-lib/aws-apigateway';
import * as iam from 'aws-cdk-lib/aws-iam';

class ApiStack extends cdk.Stack {
  constructor(scope: cdk.Construct, id: string, props?: cdk.StackProps) {
    super(scope, id, props);

    // Lambda function
    const lambdaFunction = new lambda.Function(this, 'MyApiFunction', {
      runtime: lambda.Runtime.NODEJS_14_X,
      handler: 'index.handler',
      code: lambda.Code.fromAsset('lambda'),
    });

    // API Gateway
    const api = new apigateway.RestApi(this, 'MyApi', {
      restApiName: 'My API Service',
      description: 'This service serves our API.',
    });

    // Lambda Integration
    const lambdaIntegration = new apigateway.LambdaIntegration(lambdaFunction);

    // Create a GET method on the root resource
    api.root.addMethod('GET', lambdaIntegration);

    // Outputs
    new cdk.CfnOutput(this, 'ApiUrl', {
      value: api.url ?? 'Something went wrong with the deploy',
    });
  }
}

const app = new cdk.App();
new ApiStack(app, 'ApiStack');
```

In this example:

- **Lambda function** is defined using the CDK's lambda.Function construct.
- **API Gateway** is created with the apigateway.RestApi construct.
- The Lambda function is connected to the API Gateway using a **Lambda Integration**.

15.3.5 How to Use Cloud Infrastructure Templates

1. **Set up AWS CLI and Configure Credentials**: Before deploying, ensure that AWS CLI is installed and configured with the necessary access credentials (aws configure).

2. **Write the Template/Code**: Write the CloudFormation YAML/JSON template or CDK code to define the infrastructure. Customize it to include the specific resources needed for your application.

3. **Deploy with CloudFormation**: Use the AWS CLI or AWS Management Console to deploy the CloudFormation stack:
   bash
   Copy
   ```
   aws cloudformation deploy --template-file template.yaml --stack-name my-api-stack
   ```

4. **Deploy with CDK**: Install dependencies and deploy with the CDK:
   bash
   Copy
   ```
   npm install
   ```

```
cdk deploy
```

5. **Monitor and Maintain**: Use AWS CloudWatch to monitor your resources. You can also use AWS CloudFormation StackSets to manage infrastructure across multiple regions and accounts.

15.4 Access to a Private Developer Forum for Q&A and Networking

Being part of a **developer community** can provide you with continuous learning, problem-solving assistance, and networking opportunities. A **private developer forum** is a valuable resource that connects developers working on similar projects or in the same technology stack. These forums offer **Q&A** sessions, best practice discussions, tutorials, and sometimes even job opportunities.

15.4.1 Benefits of Joining a Developer Forum

1. **Access to Expertise**: Private developer forums often feature **industry experts**, thought leaders, and experienced developers who can offer insights into best practices, complex use cases, and advanced troubleshooting.
2. **Networking Opportunities**: Being a member of a private forum provides networking opportunities that can lead to collaborations, job opportunities, and knowledge sharing within the development community.
3. **Problem-Solving**: Developer forums are perfect for getting answers to specific coding problems. The community can provide quick solutions, alternative approaches, and valuable tips that speed up the development process.
4. **Learning and Skill Building**: Forums are often a place for **continuous learning** through shared experiences, code snippets, and community-driven resources like tutorials, guides, and workshops.
5. **Exclusive Resources**: Many private forums offer exclusive resources, including:
   - **Workshops** and **seminars** hosted by experienced developers.
   - **Webinars** or video tutorials on advanced topics.
   - **Job boards** and project collaboration opportunities.

15.4.2 How to Participate in a Developer Forum

1. **Sign-Up**: Join a private developer forum relevant to your interests or technology stack. Some well-known forums include **Stack Overflow** (with premium services), **Dev.to**, and specialized Slack communities, Discord servers, or **Reddit communities**. These may require an invitation or approval for full membership.
2. **Ask Questions**: Start by introducing yourself and asking questions. Don't hesitate to ask for help on issues you're stuck on. When posting a question, provide clear context and any relevant code snippets to increase the chances of receiving quality help.
3. **Contribute**: As you gain experience, contribute by helping others. Provide feedback on their questions, share solutions, write blog posts or tutorials, and share useful resources with the community.
4. **Attend Events**: Participate in any live events such as webinars, coding challenges, or workshops. These events can help you stay updated on the latest trends and techniques in software development.

15.4.3 Examples of Popular Developer Forums

1. **GitHub Discussions**: GitHub offers a forum-like feature called **Discussions**, which enables developers to ask questions, share ideas, and collaborate on open-source projects. It's an excellent place to engage with the community around a specific technology or project.

2. **Stack Overflow** (Premium/Enterprise): Stack Overflow is one of the largest and most popular forums for developers. The **premium version** offers personalized Q&A and provides additional resources, direct access to experts, and deeper analytics.

3. **Dev.to**: Dev.to is a community-driven platform that allows developers to share articles, ask questions, and engage in discussions. It has a welcoming environment for developers of all experience levels.

4. **Slack & Discord Communities**: Many developer forums and communities are hosted on **Slack** or **Discord**, offering real-time discussions and collaboration. These are often private and invite-only, focusing on specific technologies, frameworks, or projects.

www.ingramcontent.com/pod-product-compliance
Lightning Source LLC
LaVergne TN
LVHW051324050326
832903LV00031B/3344

* 9 7 9 8 3 1 9 4 8 4 4 6 8 *